Training Your Labrador Retriever

2nd Edition

September B. Morn

BARRON'S

Cover Credits

Front cover: Shutterstock; back cover, inside front cover, inside back cover: Paulette Johnson.

Photo Credits

Kent Dannen: pages 4, 5, 8, 17, 22, 27, 29, 31 (top and bottom), 32, 33 (bottom), 34, 37, 44, 50, 51, 61, 66 (top), 73, 76, 81, 83, 85, 86, 88, 94, 96, 99, 101, 102, 104, 106, 110, 115, 116, 119, 122, 125, 127, 129, 130, 134, 137; Cheryl A. Ertelt: pages 2, 3, 12, 18, 66 (bottom), 67 (top and bottom), 68, 69, 71, 120; Shirley Fernandez/Paulette Johnson: pages 84, 89; Isabelle Francais: pages 40, 52; Daniel Johnson: pages 112, 114, 139; Paulette Johnson: pages 11, 21, 38, 43 (top), 45, 48, 54, 72, 123, 149; Pets by Paulette: pages 9, 33 (top), 79; Connie Summers/Paulette Johnson: pages 10, 16, 58, 62, 64, 65.

All inquiries should be addressed to:
Barron's Educational Series, Inc.
250 Wireless Boulevard
Hauppauge, New York 11788
www.barronseduc.com

ISBN-13: 978-0-7641-4255-0
ISBN-10: 0-7641-4255-0

Library of Congress Catalog Card No. 2009931082

Printed in China
9 8 7 6 5 4 3 2 1

Acknowledgments

When I was an infant of two weeks I met King, my grandmother's black Lab. King gave me my first doggie kisses and lessons in dog language. I dedicate this book to King, for being my first Labrador buddy.

My thanks to: Nana's King, Mom's Cinderella, and all Labs everywhere, for their optimism and affection; the hundreds of Lab owners whose questions helped frame this book; Nancy and Elizabeth Davis and "Lucy," Anara Thomas and "Sunny"; Rebecca Fischer and "Alex"; and all the folks and Labs who helped.

About the Author

September B. Morn has more than 25 years of experience as a dog trainer and behavioral consultant. She has developed adoption-enhancement training programs used by humane shelters and has testified as an expert witness in court cases involving dog aggression. She teaches classes and workshops on problem solving, manners and obedience, Rally, Agility, clicker training, Canine Good Citizen, and musical freestyle. Her dogs have appeared on the theater stage and in television commercials.

Morn has authored nine books to date and has received numerous writing awards, including four Maxwell medallions from the Dog Writers Association of America.

Contents

4 *Training Equipment* 30

5 *Leadership and Mutual Respect* 35

6 *Health* 41

1 *Labrador Retriever History*

Origins of the Labrador Retriever

The beginning of humankind's association with canines is not clearly known, but most historians agree that cubs of wild canines—probably wolves—were captured or befriended, socialized, and bred to produce tamer offspring. Individuals with desirable traits and abilities were mated and, as centuries stretched into millennia, many varied breeds of dogs came into being. Each breed was developed for a certain purpose. The Labrador Retriever was developed for retrieving in water.

The Labrador Retriever originated in Canada before 1800, not in Labrador, as the name implies, but along the east and southeast coast of Newfoundland. First known as St. John's water dogs, Labs were related to the larger, long-haired Newfoundland dogs. The St. John's water dogs were smaller, but very hardy and extremely strong swimmers. They were originally used by fishermen to retrieve codfish that managed to shake off the hook while being pulled to the surface. The dogs also helped haul ashore heavy, water-soaked nets. The advantage of the smooth coat of the St. John's dogs over the Newfies' shaggy fur was that ice did not form on the short, water-repellent hair and weigh the dog down. Black was by far the most common color for these dogs, yellow was uncommon, chocolate rare.

By the end of the 1700s St. John's water dogs were shipped to England, where they met with great favor as gundogs. Fanciers began breeding the dogs, and by 1850 they were well established in England. There is no record of who first started calling these dogs Labrador Retrievers, but the name began in England in the mid-1800s.

Note: Because Labs are such good buddies, I have given the name "Buddy" to the "universal Lab" in this book. Though a buddy could be either male or female, this Buddy happens to be a male, so in this book masculine pronouns are used when referring to the dogs (except when pertaining specifically to female Labs).

The Labrador Retriever was developed for water work.

When the Kennel Club of England was formed in 1878, all retrievers were registered simply as "retrievers." The Labrador Retriever was classified as a separate breed in 1904. English-bred Labradors arrived back in Newfoundland about that time and a Labrador Retriever club was formed there. An English import Lab won Best in Show at the first all-breed Newfoundland Kennel Club show.

Labs became popular hunting retrievers and family companions on both sides of the Atlantic and developed a reputation for hardiness, scenting ability, good temper, love of water, and careful retrieves. England's royal family began breeding Labs at their Wolferton and Sandringham kennels in the early 1900s, and continue today. Labs are used in Eng-

land as police dogs and guide dogs, as well as for hunting and companionship.

Uses
Scent Work

On this side of the Atlantic we see more German Shepherds and Rottweilers than Labradors in police patrol work, but Labs are often selected for jobs requiring scent work. Customs Service officers often use this breed to detect illegal drugs and other contraband at border crossings, seaports, and airports. Some of these dogs are donated; others are adopted from shelters. Good candidates are energetic, self-confident, and espe-

Labs are popular as hunting dogs.

cially avid game players, because Customs dogs are rewarded for finds with a rousing game of fetch or tug, for which Labradors can be perfect.

Suspicious vehicles crossing the Mexican or Canadian border into the United States may be scent-searched by a four-legged officer. Customs dogs routinely sniff at vehicle bumpers, tires, and tailpipes— favorite hiding places for contraband. Baggage at airports gets similar treatment. A dog runs along the conveyer, jumps onto each suitcase, and sniffs the slight puff of air that comes out.

A trained Lab can detect marijuana or hashish from yards away and find drugs or explosives hidden inside thick, double-walled containers. Smugglers sometimes pack fragrant materials, such as coffee or mothballs, in with drug shipments to confuse Customs dogs, but this ploy seldom works. No matter how well a smuggler thinks he or she has concealed the contraband, a Lab trained to sniff out the substance can find it.

Tracking

Another notable Labrador talent is tracking and finding lost people. Search and Rescue (SAR) trainers often choose Labs for their excellent scenting ability and their outgoing, people-friendly nature. A good SAR dog really likes people and puts his all into tracking them. If a dog does not really care much for people, he may not be sufficiently motivated to follow a difficult trail to find and rescue some

stranger. An SAR dog is trained with encouragement and rewards, which help build a strong partnership with the handler and enhance the dog's friendship and trust for people.

Assistance Dogs

Many working Labs are employed in the assistance dog field, especially as guide and service dogs. Pups are usually raised by volunteers who socialize them around people and animals in different settings and start their basic obedience training. When

A working Assistance Dog.

pups are grown they go to assistance dog school, where they are given specific training by professionals. At the end of training, each dog is teamed up with a person with a disability. The dog and his human partner then train together to develop a working relationship. A person with a disability partnered with a well-educated assistance Lab finds greater freedom with the dog's eager help. For more on careers for Labs, see pages 128–131.

Companionship

This breed remains popular with hunters, happily retrieving downed waterfowl from icy ponds and rivers, but hunting is, at most, only a seasonal occupation and most Labs find their life's work as family companions. This is a task for which the Lab's friendly, playful nature is ideally suited, as proven by their perennial popularity. The Labrador Retriever consistently rates in the top ten breeds registered by the American Kennel Club (AKC) and is, at the time of this writing, the most popular dog in the United States.

Lab Body and Mind

The official AKC Standard for the Labrador Retriever describes "a strongly built, medium-size, short-coupled dog possessing a sound, athletic, well-balanced conformation that enables him to function as a retrieving gun dog, the substance and soundness to hunt waterfowl or upland game for long hours under difficult conditions, the character and quality to win in the show ring and the temperament to be a family companion." With those qualities bred in for 300 years or so, it's no wonder the Lab's popularity endures.

The Labrador Retriever is strong-bodied and strong-willed. Whatever a Lab sets his mind to do—or not do—will receive his full energy. This can be beneficial when working with a Lab, or it can be frustrating. The Lab's energy must be properly channeled or it can easily get out of control.

From the beginning the Labrador was bred to work. With characteristic strength, energy, and enthusiasm, work is play to a Lab, but not just a frivolous game. Labs play and work with the body/mind concentration of professional athletes. They like to test their strength and will push themselves hard. This is important to remember when training, because a Lab may test himself by testing his handler's determination.

Develop a good rapport with Buddy and teach him the basics as a pup. Stay a step ahead of his tests by giving tests of your own—practice obedience commands in real-life situations. Teach Buddy how to win by pleasing you. The earlier your puppy is introduced to the exhilaration of success in training, the more readily he will cooperate with you.

Labs are normally happy and optimistic, always ready to play or make a friend. A Lab with correct temperament can be a good watchdog, barking an alarm when visitors approach, but he should not be aggressive toward people or animals. The Lab is well known for a gentle mouth and great patience, and reputable breeders are careful to maintain those traits in their lines.

Unfortunately, the Lab's consistent popularity has attracted some ignorant and unscrupulous people who breed dogs solely for profit, causing a decline in both working ability and temperament. Buyers seeking sound Labs with correct temperament as family pets, workers, or hunting companions are advised to acquire the dogs from reputable, experienced breeders.

A Lab Needs a Job

Labs are intelligent and full of energy. If nothing harnesses those traits in a positive way, Buddy will start thinking up things to do for exercise and amusement. Unemployed Labs become absorbed in such hobbies as barking, digging, bicycle chasing, fence fighting, and out-of-season hunting. Once these behaviors become habits, they can be difficult to stop; therefore, it's better to prevent the

problem by giving Buddy something constructive to do with his time and energy.

Obedience training is a good entry-level job for a Lab; it teaches a dog to control his impulses and cooperate with his handler. Obedience training lays the foundation for all other work by establishing a vocabulary of commands. Start training when Buddy is very young, using reward-based methods, and engage him in a partnership rather than a contest of wills.

Labs make excellent family companions.

5

Hunting

A traditional job for a Lab is hunting retriever. This breed shines at this work, and most take to retrieving game birds as if remembering how, rather than learning something new. Commands must be learned by voice, hand, and whistle. Complicated and multiple retrieves must be practiced; skills must be refined. A good rapport between dog and handler must be built and nurtured.

Hunting seasons often last only a few weeks, but hunting dogs are athletes and must have activity to keep them occupied and fit the rest of the year. Training for

Labs can succeed at many different jobs.

Field Trial, Obedience, Tracking, or Agility competition is a great off-season way to keep Buddy active and fit year-round.

Since many Lab owners are not hunters, less traditional jobs must be found for the dogs. Training for competition is enjoyable for some dog/handler teams, whereas others enjoy games and sports. There are numerous activities to enjoy with a breed as versatile as the Lab.

If you want to practice teamwork and help people at the same time, you and your Lab might enjoy pet-assisted therapy volunteer work. Therapy dogs visit hospitals and nursing facilities, bringing comfort and joy to shut-ins. Dogs must be healthy, gentle, friendly, steady, well mannered, and well groomed for this work. Basic obedience training and thorough socialization are essential to prepare for this rewarding occupation.

There are also everyday jobs around the home that any Lab can be trained to do. Fetching various items on command is a task many dogs enjoy. Start by teaching Buddy to retrieve his toys, then progress to other items. Dogs especially like to fetch things that make their day more fun, such as leashes, car keys, and walking shoes.

Finding a job for your Lab should not be difficult; simply choose an activity that appeals to you both and get busy. Labs have always worked for a living. It's a matter of pride.

2 Choosing Your Labrador Retriever

Which Lab for You?

A well-cared-for Labrador Retriever can live a dozen years or longer, so choose your new dog with care. If all goes well, Buddy will be your buddy for many wonderful years.

Prospective buyers may feel overwhelmed by the wide selection of Labs to pick from. Pups and adults can be obtained from breeders, shelters, rescue groups, and classified ads. With three colors, two genders, a range of ages, and show, field, and pet stock to choose from, the selection can be mind-boggling.

Which Color?

Labs come in three solid colors: black, yellow, and chocolate. No other colors are permitted by the Labrador Retriever Standard. A small spot of white on the chest is permissible but not desirable. Markings elsewhere, any other color, or a mix of colors disqualifies a Lab from the conformation ring.

Black, yellow, and chocolate pups can appear together in one litter if the parents' gene combination is right. Regardless of color, a Lab should conform to the Standard.

For more than 400 years hunters have extolled the virtues of one color retriever over another. Way back in 1621 Gervase Markham attempted to put the matter to rest in his book *Hunger's Prevention and the Whole Art of Fowling by Land and Water*, arguing that a good dog is the product of training, not color. The language is archaic, but Markham's assertion is still sound:

> First, for the Colours of the best Water Dogge; albeit some will describe more excellence to one Colour than another. . . . Yet in truth it is nothing so, for all Colours are alike. . . . Instruction is the Liquor wherewith they are seasoned and if they be well handled at the first, they will ever smell of that discretion, and if they be ill handled they will ever stink of that Folly.

Note: Coat color is not linked to body type or temperament and has nothing to do with how good a companion, hunter, or show dog a Lab will be.

Labs come in three colors: black, yellow, and chocolate.

Male or Female?

Some owners believe male dogs make better workers and females better pets; others argue the opposite, saying males are cuddlier and females more business-like. The truth is that a Lab's individual temperament matters far more than gender. Both female and male Labs can be excellent workers and playful, affectionate companions. Males often are larger and stronger than females, but the size difference does not normally hinder performance.

If you already have a dog, your new Lab will be entering claimed turf. This may cause ruffled fur and some dogs become very possessive when a new dog enters the home. Though most dogs work it out together over time, some can be quite aggressive toward a newcomer-dog. Often, dogs of opposite sex get along better than same-sex dogs. Neutering both dogs may change the potential for conflict, but does not always eliminate it. If your present dog is very bossy or territorial, you might preserve everyone's nerves by choosing a new Lab that is the opposite sex.

Two handsome Labrador pups.

What Age Is Best?

Pup, adult, or senior Lab—what age is best to adopt? The answer depends on your plans for the dog and how much energy and time you can devote. In general, the younger the dog, the more time and energy are required of owners for training, care, and exercise.

Puppies are the most labor-intensive choice. To teach confidence and good manners, considerable time must be spent training and socializing a pup. At seven or eight weeks, little Buddy needs to urinate about once an hour, although it may seem more frequent to harried new owners. If someone is home to let Buddy out when he needs to go, house-training will be more quickly accomplished. The more time a pup is left alone, the longer it will take him to learn clean habits.

The younger your pup, the more influence you'll have on his attitude and behavior, but the more time and attention you'll need to lavish on him. If you are short on time, patience, or paper towels, do yourself a big favor and don't adopt a young pup.

Adolescent Dogs

At six months to a year a dog is not as cuddly as a little pup but may be a better pet choice for a busy household. The adolescent dog's body and mind are well developed, and his physical needs are less urgent than a pup's. At this age Buddy can tolerate four to six hours a day alone (in a puppy-proof area).

An adolescent Lab may already have learned decent manners and some have had formal training. Although an adolescent dog from a loving home may miss his former family at first, he will readily adapt to a new home when given affection and attention. In a few weeks, an adolescent dog can bond to a loving new family.

Labs that have formerly been neglected, or even abused, can recover with a caring and patient new owner. An underappreciated dog has probably heard his name used often in anger. You can

help your new Lab forget his unhappy past by giving him a fresh start with a brand new name. Drop the old, tainted "bad dog" name and use the new name whenever you praise, play with, pet, or feed him. In a week or less, Buddy will respond proudly to his new name.

Adolescent dogs have abundant energy and require lots of exercise to stay out of trouble. A walk around the block is not enough for a big young Lab; he also needs to run and play. Since the Lab's heritage is to retrieve, *fetch* games are natural for exercise. If Buddy is sociable with other dogs, make play dates with his friends from obedience class or visit an off-leash park a few times a week so he can romp with other dogs.

Mental activity is also vital for a young dog, as bored adolescents can become destructive and unruly. Challenge Buddy's mind with activities that make him think.

- Enroll in obedience lessons and practice homework every day.
- Teach tricks and games.
- Join an Agility class or musical freestyle group.
- Discover what interests Buddy and include that in his training as an activity and a reward; for example, keep interest high for a dog that likes to play catch by sometimes rewarding a good *stay* position by tossing him a ball.

Make sure your adolescent Lab has plenty of toys to gnaw when left alone. Since young Labs feel the need to exercise their growing teeth and jaws, they need plenty of interesting, satisfying chew toys to prevent damage to other objects such as walls, floors, furniture, and so on. Toys

Your Lab needs the proper toys from puppy to adult.

Adopting a mature Lab can be very rewarding.

that hold and intermittently dispense food are excellent and can keep a dog occupied chewing for hours (see page 78). If you use two or three food-dispensing toys and vary their contents, Buddy's interest in the toys will remain high.

Adult Dogs

Adopting a mature dog can be very rewarding. Some mature dogs adapt to new owners more quickly than others, but most form strong new loyalties within two or three months. Adults demand less time and energy than pups or adolescents, and may already be quite well trained; however, even if your new Lab has very good manners, you'd be wise to take him through a positive-motivation obedi- ence course (see page 59) to ease his adjustment.

Adult Labs may be rather set in their ways, but patient training can change that. Some behaviors are more durable than others; for instance, house soiling and aggression toward people or animals are problems that may require assistance from a professional. Ask your veterinarian for a referral to a trainer experienced in working with difficult behavior.

> **Caution:** Don't let Buddy play with too many friends at one time; it's fun, but it can be dangerous for a mob of dogs to wrestle.

To Breed or Neuter?

Unless Buddy is part of a well-planned breeding program, neutering is the most logical option. A neutered dog is usually more steady because no fluctuating sex hormones take over control of the dog's brain. Neutered dogs also tend to live longer because they are protected against cancers and diseases that attack the reproductive system.

Neutered males do not tend to fight with other dogs as intact ones do, saving

A mother Labrador nurses her litter.

injuries and social embarrassment. Spayed females, obviously, do not become pregnant. Pregnancy and reproductive disease are far more serious health risks than spaying. Some spayed females experience urinary incontinence because of hormone imbalance, but this problem can be corrected with medication.

Where to Find a Lab

All Labs are not created equal, so buyer beware! Quality may vary tremendously from source to source and price does not always accurately reflect a dog's value. Learn all you can before you select a dog. Information is your ally.

Breeders

There are knowledgeable breeders for whom Labradors are their life's passion and who breed primarily to produce increasingly better dogs. Unfortunately, not all breeders are concerned with quality. There are disreputable people who cash in on breed popularity, producing pups with unsound bodies and temperaments. How can you sort the good breeders from the not so good? It's actually easier than you might think.

A reputable breeder's dogs will be certified clear of serious joint and eye defects and will have proven their quality in the field and/or show ring. The dogs' ancestors will also have worked and/or earned titles in competition.

Reputable breeders will ask potential owners many questions about home, family, lifestyle, and other pets before agreeing to place a dog with them. They will offer a written contract spelling out the responsibilities of buyer and seller, including a provision arranging the fate of the dog should the placement not work satisfactorily. An experienced breeder will send home pages of instructions with each dog placed and will maintain contact with buyers, offering help and advice throughout the life of the dog.

The reputable breeder's dogs are carefully bred, healthy and sound, immunized, well groomed, and socialized. When you obtain a dog from a reputable breeder, regardless of the price tag, the dog is a bargain.

Breed Rescue

Labrador breed clubs organize volunteers to rescue Labs from homelessness, neglect, and abuse. Responsible breeders who support these efforts often chair the rescue groups, and volunteer much private time, money, and kennel space to help the dogs.

Lab Rescue takes in dogs of all ages, but usually has fewer pups than adults. If you are a little flexible about the age of your new dog, Lab Rescue may have the perfect Lab for you (see Useful Addresses and Literature, page 142). Dogs placed by Rescue are neutered, and many receive rehabilitative training and care before they are ready for new homes.

Rescue Labs may or may not come from titled ancestors, but adoptive owners are

treated the same way as buyers for show pups. If you adopt from Rescue, be prepared to answer personal questions about yourself, your home, and your family. Rescue groups want what's best for the dogs, and volunteers will do all they can to make certain a new home works out right.

Shelters and Pounds

Many stray or unwanted Labs sit in shelters awaiting adoption. Sometimes, well-loved dogs are rehomed through shelters; others end up there when irresponsible owners tire of them. Some have been abused and neglected by the time they are dropped off at the "pound." Although some shelter dogs bounce back easily from earlier hardship, others have behavior problems that will require time and training to correct.

Most shelter dogs make wonderful companions once they learn to trust new owners. Though they may require extra patience and care at first, most shelter adoptees give back a thousandfold in devotion to a loving family.

What Influences a Dog's Temperament?

Environment

Early life experiences affect a dog's ability to trust people and handle stress. A good environment is one that provides positive social experiences and teaches a pup to make friends with people and animals. Quarters should be kept clean and the pup's mind stimulated with toys and household sounds, sights, and smells. Positive socialization enables a pup to confidently adapt to new situations.

Heredity

Most people realize that size and color are hereditary, but fewer understand that temperament and working ability are also passed through the genes. Pups can inherit such temperament problems as shyness or aggression. For this reason, you should try to meet the sire and dam of any pup you consider for adoption. If you cannot meet the parents or close relatives, at least study the pedigree carefully.

Interpreting a Pedigree

A pedigree is a genealogy chart, the written record of a dog's ancestry. Pedigrees are arranged by generation, with the sire's name listed above the dam's. Included with names of ancestors are their show and working titles. Some pedigrees also list colors and health clearances or certifications. Simply having a pedigree does not necessarily mean a dog is the product of careful breeding; it merely means the dog has a traceable lineage. To know whether a dog's pedigree is good you must know how to interpret it.

■ At the left of the document, on a line by itself, is the name of the dog whose pedigree you're examining. To the right of that are his sire and dam. To their right are his grandparents, and so on, back through the generations. The farther to the right a dog's name appears in the pedigree, the less genetic impact it has on your pup. The same dog may appear several times in a pedigree, multiplying that dog's genetic influence.

■ The letters before or after the names in a pedigree are abbreviations for titles earned. Championships are listed before the name, and performance titles after it. Take a hypothetical example: DUAL CH. Buddy Ombudsman O'Budd, CDX, TD. Translation? Buddy has earned both Field and Conformation Championships, the Companion Dog Excellent obedience title, and the Tracking Dog title. From this we may gather that Buddy is a wonderful all-around Lab—beautiful, sound, smart, and obedient. We know this because he could not otherwise have earned those letters.

There is an old saying: "Breed the best to the best, then hope for the best." That's what responsible breeders do, and that's what to look for in a pedigree. Not every Lab with titled parents and grandparents turns out to be a star, of course, but the odds are far better with a background of champions and performance dogs than with unproved stock.

3 The First Month with Your New Lab

The Bonding Period

The first month with Buddy will be an important bonding period. You and he will get to know each other and settle into a routine. New experiences leave durable impressions on a pup, so your first month together is prime time to train him. It's much easier to teach good habits than erase bad ones, so help Buddy learn good habits from his first day home.

Puppies absorb new information like sponges, so you need to start training Buddy right away, whatever his age. Since a puppy's attention span is shorter than that of an adult, keep the sessions short. Realistic expectations will minimize frustration and maximize the important first month with Buddy.

Teaching Rules and Limits

All dogs need proper guidance to learn acceptable behavior in a new household. Some new dog owners think they should ease a dog's transition by waiting until he settles in before introducing rules, but

that is no favor for a new dog trying to learn the laws that govern your pack.

Setting no rules at first, then suddenly forbidding behavior you've previously allowed will confuse your dog; he will not understand why the rules have suddenly changed. It is kinder and more effective to enforce reasonable limits from the beginning. Show Buddy how you want him to behave, then praise good manners. Keep an eye on Buddy and guide him to chew appropriate toys and eliminate in approved areas. When you cannot watch him, use gates, fences, and crates to keep him safely away from forbidden items and places.

Dogs learn, whether or not we actively train them, taking their cues from what we do and what we allow them to do. It is your responsibility to teach Buddy good habits. If you slack off on supervision and management while Buddy is getting to know your rules, any mischief he gets into will be your fault, not his.

House-training

House-training is one of the big challenges faced by new dog owners. Elimination rules should be introduced as soon as you

A pup needs to eliminate soon after he eats, drinks, plays, or wakes from a nap.

bring Buddy home. You'll do best if you've planned ahead for his arrival, with an elimination area selected before he arrives.

Dogs from responsible sources will have been housed in sanitary quarters since birth. This encourages them to keep themselves clean and makes house-training easier. Weaned pups from clean homes will move away from eating and sleeping areas to eliminate. Make this easy for Buddy by placing his food bowl and bed at least 6 feet (1.8 m) from his relief area.

There are certain predictable times that dogs, especially puppies, will need to eliminate: after they eat or drink, when they wake, after an exciting event, and when they pause in play. A pup gives clues when he needs to urinate or defecate. He may seem restless, sniff the ground, circle, or start to leave the area. Quickly take him where you want him to eliminate and stand by patiently, ready to praise.

Older pups and adults may already be clean in the house, but some have lived only outdoors and must be trained by the new owner. House-training adults is similar to house-training pups, but adults have better control so timing of outings is less critical. Learn Buddy's elimination patterns and be attentive to his body language so you can anticipate his needs and take him outside at the proper times.

House-soiling Problems

Some dogs, instead of asking to go out, will sneak off to a little-used room and soil there. There is a good reason for this. The room at the far end of the hall may seem, to a dog, suitably remote to use for relief, like an indoor backyard. This frustrates owners, but the dog is basically on the right track—trying to avoid soiling the main living area. He needs help to understand that the only approved relief place is outdoors.

Until Buddy's house manners are reliable, you should not allow him free run of your house. Keep him with you like a shadow, leashed to your belt if necessary, so he cannot wander off and make mistakes in other parts of the house. This enforced proximity offers opportunities to teach basic obedience skills, such as *sit*, *down*, and *stay*, in the context of good house manners.

Dogs naturally avoid soiling their sleeping area, so a crate-den (see page 18) can help with house-training. When crated, a pup or dog will make a fuss, asking to be let out when he needs to eliminate. A pup raised in an unclean environment may soil his crate because he has never known cleanliness. This will take time and lots of patience to correct. When a dog messes in his crate, it is usually because he couldn't help it, so never scold or punish. Be sure to give Buddy a good opportunity to empty out before you put him in his crate-den. Patience, not punishment, is the key to house-training.

Most dogs will try to stay clean once they understand the rules. If you think Buddy is taking too long to house-train or if, once trained, he begins soiling again, consult your veterinarian. Before you assume Buddy is willfully messing, make certain he's physically able to be house-trained. Slowness to house-train can be a sign of bladder or bowel problems; a dog with cystitis, for example, may have urine accidents repeatedly, even though you've been very clear with teaching rules. A "stubborn" pup may actually be ill. Be sure before you scold.

Confinement

When Buddy must spend time alone you should confine him for his own protection. While his owner's back is turned, a puppy can get into five no-no's in four minutes. To prevent Buddy from hurting himself or damaging your belongings, confine him when you must leave him unattended. Three good options for indoor confinement are baby gates, exercise pens ("ex-pens"), and crates.

A Puppy Corral

In general, the more family traffic through or near the pup's area, the better, as this provides better socialization opportunities; therefore, the kitchen is usually the best spot for a puppy corral. Puppies need plenty of social interaction or they may become shy or aggressive. A pup should spend at least five hours a day around people; he needs to be close to activity to feel included in the pack.

Baby gates across the doorways can turn your kitchen or laundry room into a puppy corral. Remember that puppies explore the world with nose and mouth, with no regard for consequences, and can consume ant poison, cleanser, steel wool, and other dangerous items. Do a thorough safety check before leaving your pup in his corral. Disaster prevention is your responsibility.

If you'd prefer not to give over your entire kitchen to Buddy, you might limit his area with a folding exercise pen. Ex-pens, as they're called, make excellent

A pup is safe in an exercise pen.

A crate is a dog's cozy private space.

temporary puppy corrals either indoors or out. They are easy to set up and take down, fold flat for storage, and can be linked together to form a larger enclosure.

If you must leave a young pup alone for more than a half hour, you may expect him to eliminate in his puppy corral. Put an area of newspapers or commercial puddle pads where you want him to relieve himself in his enclosure. Place crate, food, and water as far away as possible from the elimination area.

Crates

Dogs enjoy lounging in cozy, protected spots that are out of the main area of household traffic, yet offer a view of the goings-on. In nature a dog would have to find or make a cozy den, but we can provide a dog crate as a civilized den substitute. Crate-dens made of wire panels or opaque molded plastic come in sizes to accommodate any breed. Most dogs like crates, once they become accustomed to them.

Plastic crates are molded in two sections that fasten together. Their smooth interior surface is comfortable for the dog, and most are safety-approved for airline travel. Wire crates are airier than plastic and also noisier (panels rattle); their advantage is that they fold flat for storage. Some wire crates come decorated with a rattan look that makes them seem more like furniture. Wire crates are not meant for air travel.

There are other crate styles as well:

- One made of heavy, rigid, plastic mesh that folds for storage.
- Heavy-duty shipping crates made of wood or metal; strong, but awkward to store or carry.
- Lightweight, collapsible fabric crates; the fabric can be destroyed by a rowdy dog, so should be used only for those dogs that are calm and already crate-trained.

Crate-training

To crate-train your Lab, set up the crate where he can explore it. Leave the door off or tie it open. Toss in a few tasty tidbits and a chew toy and let him explore the crate on his own.

When Buddy is comfortable in the crate with the door open, you can close the door for a moment with him inside. Feed him his meals in the crate, closing the door while he eats and letting him out when he is finished. Build pleasant associations and soon he will have no anxiety about the crate.

"Instant" Crate-training

You can crate-train a dog in one day, if necessary. Start by allowing Buddy to explore the crate, as explained above. After he has gone in and out a few times, close the door for a moment. Talk to him pleasantly; be matter-of-fact and upbeat. Do not pity or commiserate or Buddy will

think something is wrong with being in the crate.

After a few minutes, let him out. Encourage him to go in and out a few more times. Put a chew toy in the crate and close the door for ten minutes. Later that day, feed him dinner in the crate.

An hour before your normal bedtime, take Buddy out to relieve himself one last time, then put the crate beside your bed and close Buddy in with a nylon or rubber (quiet) chew toy. You'll probably need that extra hour to settle Buddy if he decides not to accept the crate. Put on some soft music and go to bed. Reassure the pup once or twice that you are right there. Don't be apologetic; if you give in, crate-training will be much harder.

How Long Can a Dog Be Crated?

A pup can stay in his crate all night, with one mid-sleep outing for younger ones. During the day, a pup should not be left crated for more than one hour per month of age. This means that a two-month-old puppy can be crated no longer than two hours. No dog should be crated for more than five hours of the day.

A crate is great for keeping Buddy safe and out of mischief while you shower, dress, or run errands, but for longer periods, a fenced yard or puppy corral should be used instead. A young Lab needs to exercise and play during the day and will need to eliminate every couple of hours. If you must leave Buddy alone for more than a few hours, confine him in the puppy corral with toys, food, water, and relief papers.

Pet Doors

One of the biggest house-training aids is a pet door to make your dog's toileting area easily accessible to him. Pet doors speed house-training by allowing Buddy to let himself out when he needs to go. They can be installed easily in most doors, including sliding glass doors, and even in walls. Most have a plastic flap that the dog pushes open with his nose, but that blocks wind and weather from entering your home. Most pet doors have a panel that slides into place to keep the door closed when you wish to limit Buddy's access. Of course, pet doors are safe only when they open into a fenced yard.

To teach Buddy to use a pet door, stand on one side of the door with him on the other. Reach through the flap and give Buddy a treat, then show another tidbit and encourage him to step through the opening. When Buddy confidently goes through with the flap open, encourage him to operate the pet door on his own. Push the flap open at one corner and show him a treat, then pull your hand and the treat back through. Encourage him to push the flap to earn the treat. Once Buddy can operate the pet door, he can let himself in and out.

Fences, Kennels, Tie-outs

Labrador Retrievers need plenty of exercise to develop both muscle and mind. Most Labs would rather go look for a game than hang around waiting for one to start; on their own, they would head for a field to follow some trails, then hit the beach for a swim and a roll in something smelly. Unfortunately, free-spirited adventures can be dangerous for dogs. This means that Buddy might stay home only if he's securely confined.

A well-fenced yard is the ideal solution to confining a dog. Although a kennel run is fairly secure for part-time confinement, it isolates a dog and lonely dogs vent their frustration through barking, digging, and other unpleasant behavior. A fenced yard attached to your house lets Buddy feel part of the family and helps avoid isolation problems. Fence your yard to include a door of your house so Buddy can easily come in and out without feeling isolated from the family. This will help make him better adjusted and better behaved.

If your housing situation precludes an actual visible fence, the electronic variety might suit your needs. Electronic fence systems require the dog to wear a collar that emits an audible tone, warning him not to cross the boundary, and it gives him a shock if he does cross. It requires a training period for a dog to learn the boundaries and understand the consequences of crossing them. Some Labs are so body-hard that the mild shock will not deter escape. Electronic fences have some drawbacks. The collar unit can malfunction and shock a dog when he has not disobeyed the boundary; batteries can unexpectedly go dead and cause the fence to fail; free-roaming dogs can cross the electronic boundary and pick a fight with Buddy; and, of course, electronic fences offer no deterrent to human mischief makers or thieves. An electronic fence may be the best solution for some, but it is not as secure as a "real" fence.

Chain, cable, or rope tie-outs are the least secure way to keep Buddy home and should be considered only temporary confinement as they will break if not regularly untangled and maintained. In some locales it is illegal to tie or chain a dog for any reason, and the dog can be confiscated and the owner fined. The sweep of a chain or cable can injure a person or dog. As tie-outs do not prevent other animals from attacking, and a playful visitor could cause your Lab to become entangled, possibly fatally, a fenced yard is a better solution.

Give your Lab appropriate chew toys.

Dog-proofing Your House and Yard

Before you leave Buddy alone in the yard, you must dog-proof the outdoor area he will use. Puppies and many adults like to dig and chew. Labs are strong and can be quite destructive without meaning to be, damaging property and endangering themselves. Check your yard for accessible electrical wires, poisons, toxic plants, sagging fences, and loose gates. Find the hazards before Buddy does.

Anticipating and Avoiding Hazards

Dogs are optimistic creatures and seldom worry about getting hurt as they romp through life. A moment of careless curiosity can cause lasting injury, however, so we must protect our dogs from danger. With foreknowledge and preparation, most hazards can be minimized or eliminated.

Ingestible Hazards

From six weeks of age to ten months or a year Buddy may seem like a chewing machine. First he learns to use his sharp baby teeth and practices on fingers, toys, TV remotes, eyeglasses, upholstery, houseplants, rugs, and a surprising variety of other things. At four months, when permanent teeth begin to erupt, to help his baby teeth fall out and new teeth come in properly, he continues to chew all of the above, plus furniture legs, arms of people, corners of walls and stairs, and anything else he can fit in his mouth. By seven months Buddy's adult teeth are all in, but his chewing needs continue as his jaw muscles develop their adult strength. If Buddy hasn't yet learned to chew approved-only

Pups will get into all kinds of things.

items by now, he may cause considerable property damage. To prevent this, start in right away teaching your puppy what he is and isn't allowed to chew (see pages 24–25, Home and Garden Dangers).

Dogs of all ages chew. It keeps their teeth clean, gives them something to do, and provides a certain amount of exercise. Chewing creates problems only when a dog chews on our belongings instead of his own. Dogs just follow nature, chewing whatever they find, until we educate them to chew only appropriate items. It is our responsibility to prevent unfortunate chewing incidents.

There is no logic in what a dog might chew. Many nonfood items seem to please the canine palate. Puppies, especially, dis-

cover the world by eating as much of it as possible.

Toxic substances: Some toxic substances, antifreeze for example, have flavors that dogs like. Even a small amount of antifreeze can be fatal, and its sweet taste attracts dogs to drink it from roadway puddles. Slug bait and rat poisons are other tasty toxins that can kill a dog or cat. If you use any of these products, be sure to protect companion animals—and children!—from accidentally ingesting them.

Foods: Even some ordinary foods can cause harm.

■ Fatty or spicy foods can damage a dog's pancreas.

- Excessive salt can harm the kidneys.
- Chocolate or coffee can cause dangerously accelerated heartbeat.
- Cooked bones can cause blockages or perforate the intestines.
- Alcohol can permanently damage the liver.
- Xylitol, a sugar substitute commonly used in gums, candies, and toothpastes, can cause liver failure.
- Raisins and grapes can cause kidney failure.
- Onions can cause an irreversible type of anemia.
- Macadamia nuts can cause weakness, staggering, and dangerously elevated heart rate and temperature.

It's truly a wonder that dogs ever survived in the past, when all they ate was what they could mooch from the master's table.

Nonfood items: Then there are the obviously nonfood items some dogs will swallow. The amazing list of indigestible objects Labs have eaten includes, but is not limited to, coins, rings, rocks, socks, screws, needles, tacks, bolts, bullets, and batteries. As you go about hazard-proofing your home and yard, remember that just because something doesn't look like food to you, it doesn't mean Buddy won't eat it. Puppies are at greatest risk for ingesting dangerous items, but any dog might taste-test his environment. Prevention of disaster is up to you.

Prevention

To check for potential hazards, try looking at the world from Buddy's eyeview. Get down on your hands and knees, at dog height, and look around. You may be surprised how different the world looks. You'll see the bottom of tables instead of the top, shoes under beds will seem larger than life, and wastebaskets serve up delectable trash right at nose level. If you see something interesting, delicate, or dangerous down there at dog level, you can be certain Buddy will discover it too. You must move temptations out of reach or secure them some other way.

There are commercially available bitter-tasting sprays and pastes that make items less appealing to chew. If the dog gets a taste of the bitter stuff, the object may lose its appeal. Also, if he has a good-tasting chew toy available, he will most likely learn to prefer that over the treated object. Following application directions on the package, apply the product to items Buddy has been chewing that he shouldn't. Provide interesting chew toys or bones to keep his mouth busy and happy and he should leave your stuff alone.

You can prevent many eating or chewing disasters by not allowing a new dog full run of your home when unattended. There are simply too many things a curious dog could get into. Confine Buddy while you're away or asleep so he doesn't form bad house habits, and let him wander around the house only when someone can supervise him.

Teaching Not to Chew

If you teach Buddy to chew on approved items, he will cause less damage to other things. There are excellent chew toys that hold food inside and release bits of the food intermittently as the dog chews and plays. This type of toy encourages the dog to continue chewing in order to get more goodies. Chewing and turning the toy over and over, trying to get food out, provides a satisfying activity. It prevents destructive behaviors by keeping the dog's jaws too busy to chew on your belongings.

When Buddy does chew something he shouldn't, take it away and replace it with one of his toys. Labs can be willful when they really want something and Buddy may repeatedly chew a forbidden object. You'll make a big impression if, after you take away the object, you spank the object (*not* the dog!) while saying *"Noooo! Noooooo! Noooooo!"* Follow the dramatic scene by encouraging Buddy, using a pleasant voice and manner, to chew on his own toy.

Buddy may think you've gone mad—and your neighbors might too, if they see your performance—but the drama will be memorable for Buddy. The next time he considers chewing that item, he may change his mind!

Exploring and Escaping

Exploration and experimentation are signs of intelligence in dogs. A smart Lab that is left alone all day will undoubtedly look for things to do for entertainment and exercise. If there's nothing to do at home, or if something more interesting is going on nearby, Buddy may decide to seek adventure down the road. Although a good fence can control a dog's access to hazards, it will not stop his drive to explore.

To help Buddy satisfy his healthy urge to discover, you should provide daily,

monitored opportunities to explore safe areas around home and on walks. With you in attendance, Buddy can satisfy his need for adventure safely. Sharing these explorations will bond you more closely and help keep Buddy content and, consequently, less inclined to roam.

Home and Garden Dangers

As mentioned, dogs are wizards at finding hazards and then diving right in, and puppies are notorious for poisoning themselves while innocently taste-testing the environment. A number of poisonous substances are commonly found around the home. The best time to discover these toxic time bombs is before Buddy does.

The following is a list of common toxic plants and their most poisonous parts. Not every poisonous plant is included; there are many others. If Buddy chews a plant or mushroom that you think may be toxic, collect a sample if you can and call your veterinarian right away.

Flower Garden Toxins

Flower	Toxic Part
Autumn crocus	Bulbs
Bleeding heart	Foliage, roots
Castor bean	Seeds
Foxglove	Leaves
Hyacinth	Bulbs
Iris	Underground rhizomes
Larkspur	Young plant, seeds

Lily of the valley	Leaves, flowers
Monkshood	Fleshy roots
Narcissus, Daffodil	Bulbs
Star of Bethlehem	Leaves, flowers
Sweet pea	Seeds

Vegetable Garden Toxins

Vegetable	Toxic Part
Potato	All green parts
Rhubarb	Leaves
Tomato	Leaves

Ornamental Toxins

Flower	Toxic Part
Azalea, Rhododendron	All parts
Daphne	All parts, especially berries
Golden chain	Beanlike seeds
Holly	Berries
Magnolia	Flower
Wisteria	Seeds, pods
Yew	Berries, foliage

Toxic Trees and Shrubs

Tree/Shrub	Toxic Part
Black Locust	Bark, sprouts, seeds, leaves
Cherry	Twigs, leaves (especially when wilted)
Elderberry	Bark, shoots, leaves, red berries
Oaks	Leaves, acorns

Toxic House Plants

Plant	Toxic Part
Dieffenbachia	All parts
Oleander	All parts
Poinsettia	Leaves, flowers
Mistletoe	All parts

The Dangers of Swimming Pools

A Lab's love of water can get him into serious trouble if he has access to a swimming pool. The dog may jump right in, have a little fun in the water, then get tired of paddling around and decide to get out. That's the problem—there may be no way for him to get out. The dog will swim around in a panic looking for a means of escape. He may try putting his paws on the edge and pulling himself up, but this will only exhaust him as he falls back in, again and again. Labs are strong swimmers, but they can drown if trapped in an inescapable pool.

A vertical pool ladder built into the wall can be difficult or impossible for a dog to climb. A set of stairs or a floating ramp from the edge of the pool down into the water makes a pool safer, but even that won't help unless Buddy knows where they are. Mark the top of the pool steps with a potted plant or other large permanent object that's readily visible from water level at any point in the pool, and teach Buddy that that's where the exit is.

If you have a pool, the simplest way to prevent tragedy is to build a secure fence around it. You could also install a ladder at an angle Buddy could climb. Teach him where the ladder or steps are located in the pool and how to climb out. Even with a safety ladder or steps, however, Buddy should never be allowed access to your pool unless you are with him.

If you have no swimming pool, but worry that Buddy may go next door and use the neighbor's, you must find a secure way to keep him home. An ounce of prevention may be worth a pound of cure, but preventing a tragic drowning is much better than a *"cure"* that comes too late.

Safety Commands

The word *"No"* is an all-purpose word dog owners often overuse. The problem with having only this one command for all things we want a dog not to do is that it does not inform the dog what he should do. To be safe, Buddy should learn specific commands to stop and hold still, not touch something, and come away from enticing distractions. Having these more specific commands will improve communications. These concepts are not difficult to teach and can save your dog's life.

Wait

This command means *"Stop. Stand still!"* It is useful at crossings and when entering or leaving a room, car, or fenced yard. When you command *"Wait!"* Buddy should stop immediately, until you tell him to go again. You could use a different command if you prefer, such as *"Whoa,"* but not *"Stay,"* because that's a slightly different, more formalized, concept that you'll also teach. Practice *"Wait"* on leash at first, then later do it off leash.

To teach it, as you walk along, suddenly freeze and say *"Wait!"* Pronounce the command as if one more step would carry Buddy over the rim of the Grand Canyon to a tragic end. Most dogs will automatically freeze if you halt abruptly and say *"Wait!"* with the proper urgency. It's startling, so reassure Buddy by praising

and patting when he freezes in place. After a moment command *"Okay, walk."*

If Buddy does not immediately wait on command, step backward instead of just stopping. If Buddy stops, but then starts to move away as you go to pet him, take up the slack in the leash as you approach him. This teaches that he cannot go forward after *"Wait"* until you give a release command such as *"Okay, walk."*

Leave It

Most Labs are quick to gobble anything tasty they find. This can be dangerous, so control Buddy's inclination to eat or explore things he shouldn't by teaching him to *"Leave it."* First have Buddy sit and lie down a few times for treat rewards to remind him that he can earn treats by doing what you tell him to do (see pages 64 and 65 for these commands). Hold a treat in your closed fist. Say *"Leave it,"* and rest your fist on your leg. Buddy will probably "mug" your hand, sniffing, nudging, nibbling, or pawing you, trying to get at the treat. Don't let him get it. If he's very pushy, withdraw your hand and wait five seconds, then start over. When Buddy stops mugging your hand, open your fist, say *"Take it,"* and give him the treat as a reward. Do this step several

> **Note:** If Buddy growls and refuses to let go of objects he wants to keep, you should seek the help of a professional trainer.

Practice on leash first, then off leash as well.

times, until Buddy no longer tries to get at the treat in your fist.

Next, place the treat on your leg, cover it with your hand, and say *"Leave it."* When Buddy stops trying to get it, pick it up and hand it to him, saying *"Take it."* NEVER allow Buddy to eat the *leave it* bait until you give it to him and say *"Take it."*

Next, cover the treat with your hand, say *"Leave it,"* and then lift your hand to expose the treat. If Buddy goes for it, cover it immediately, repeat the *leave it* command and try uncovering it again. If Buddy doesn't move toward the treat, say *"Take it,"* and reward him with a fresh treat,

leaving the "bait" treat on your leg. Cover and uncover it several times, saying *"Leave it"* each time. Reward with a fresh treat each time he obeys. Next, place a treat on the floor and say *"Leave it."* Quickly cover it with your foot if Buddy moves toward it. When he obeys, reward with treats from your hand, leaving the bait on the floor. If Buddy moves toward the bait after eating the reward treat, say *"Leave it,"* and reward him when he obeys. Stand up and repeat the previous step.

Progress to dropping a treat, then multiple treats. Practice walking Buddy past food and other tempting stuff (first on leash, then loose). Make a habit of practicing and rewarding "*leave it*" whenever you encounter trash or other tempting no-no's when you're out and about with Buddy.

Come Away

It can be difficult to get a dog to come to you when he's busy doing something else he enjoys, so you must teach Buddy that coming when called has many benefits. With the Lab's love of food and play, *come away* is not hard to teach.

The informal *come away* does not require Buddy to sit in front of you, merely to come close enough to receive a treat and be captured (see page 62 for instructions for the formal recall and finish). Teach *come away* on leash; later you will be able to call Buddy away from distractions off lead as well.

While Buddy is enjoying an interesting scent, or being petted by a friend, or playing with another dog, call "*Buddy, come away!*" in a happy voice. Move away from him as you do this; the leash will assure that Buddy moves toward you. Praise "*Good come away!*" and give a treat. As you give the tidbit, grasp Buddy's collar with your other hand. This accustoms him to being "*caught*," which, when paired with a yummy, isn't so bad.

After you reward and praise Buddy, allow him to return to his fun. He will soon realize the win-win nature of this command: He learns to leave something he likes to get something he likes even more and then return to his fun. Very rewarding!

When Buddy masters *come away* on leash, start practicing off leash. At first

train only in enclosed areas, in case he decides to run off instead of come. If Buddy ignores your call, you'll know he still needs more leash practice.

Safety in and Around Vehicles

Teach Buddy to wait for a command before getting in or out of a vehicle. Before opening the car door, command Buddy to "*Wait.*" Stop him immediately if he disobeys and make him wait until you tell him "*Okay, hop in!*" Leash Buddy at first when teaching this; later try the lesson without the leash.

The safest way for a young puppy to ride in a vehicle is in his plastic crate-den. Seat-belt the puppy's crate next to you, with the opening toward you. The crate will limit what the pup sees, preventing overexcitement. Crate travel will teach Buddy to be a calm passenger.

Another way to keep Buddy safe while traveling is to use a seat belt/harness avail-

Note: Using a single rope to tie a dog in the back of a truck can prove fatal if he falls over the rail and is dragged. Cross-tying with two cables can prevent tragedies caused by one-rope tying, but it's still not as safe as a travel crate. A good, lockable canopy and a well-fastened crate are the safest way to transport a dog in a truck.

able from pet supply dealers. In case of sudden stops or turns, he will be held securely in place. No dog should ride loose in the back of a truck; he could be injured or killed by sliding hard into the side rail or being thrown out onto the road.

Most Labs love to go for rides and may get excited when they see dogs or other animals along the road. Teach Buddy to be calm and quiet in the car, starting when he's young. If he already has some unpleasant or dangerous travel habits, you should teach him safer manners. Work with an assistant, so one person can drive while the other trains.

Your Lab's ID

Buddy's identification tag, tattoo, or microchip is an important link to you. He should never leave home without an ID tag that contains your phone number. When vacationing with Buddy, use water-proof ink to write your local contact number on a piece of cloth tape and affix it to his ID tag. Official license tags, though required in most areas, are not sufficient to locate a dog's owner when city hall is closed. If the jingle of Buddy's ID and license tags bothers you, tape them together. That will also prevent tags from rubbing information off each other.

Tattoos are a good way to identify a dog. Many breeders tattoo newborn pups with numbers and letters that individually identify them; other owners have their dogs tattooed as adolescents or adults. Tattoos are usually placed on the inner flank or the inner upper thigh. Sometimes

A seat belt/harness will hold your dog in place while traveling in a vehicle.

the ears are tattooed instead. In some countries a tattoo is necessary to identify a purebred dog for registration and breeding purposes. Tattooing is fairly inexpensive and most dogs will allow it without sedation.

Microchip ID A tiny microchip, about the size of a rice grain, is injected just under the dog's skin between his shoulder blades. The chip stays there for life and can be read with digital scanners at most animal shelters and veterinary clinics. For a small fee national registries will record microchip numbers and tattoos so owners can be tracked down and quickly reunited with lost dogs.

4 *Training Equipment*

Training equipment of various types fills superstores and catalogs to overflowing. Such a huge assortment to choose from can seem daunting to new dog owners. There are so many different collars and leashes available that to try them all would take years. That will not be necessary, though, because a few basic pieces of equipment are really all you will need to begin training your Lab.

Collars

Your Lab's collar allows you to train him, control him, and keep him safe. There are different types of collars for different purposes. They come in cloth, leather, or metal. Some are fancy; some are plain. Some are gentle on the dog's neck; others are designed to control the dog through pain. Here is a brief description of several types of collars in popular usage.

Flat Collars

This type is usually a flat strip of nylon or leather that fastens around the dog's neck with a buckle or clasp. They are used for general wear and some types of training, and are good for hanging ID tags on.

Dogs that pull hard on lead need some other type of collar, because the flat collar places all the pulling force directly on the trachea, making it difficult to breathe, and it can damage a dog's windpipe.

Slip "Choke" Collar

This is a plain length of chain, leather, or fabric with a ring at each end. To use it as a collar, hold one of the rings in your right hand—this will be the "dead ring"—and work the rest of the collar length through. Hold the collar up so that, as you face Buddy, the collar forms the letter "P." If it looks like a "9" instead, turn it around or it will be put on the dog the wrong way. Slip the "P" over Buddy's head as you face him. The working ring should be against the right side of his neck. That way the collar will pull closed and release properly with Buddy at *heel* on your left (to learn the *heel* command, see page 62).

Slip collars are used in training, but they are also often misused. This looks like a simple tool, but improper use is more common than owners realize. Never permit a dog to wear any slip-type collar unsupervised, as it could become caught on something and strangle him.

Never pull a slip collar tight and keep it tight; you could harm the dog. The proper action is a light, quick pull and release.

Damage to neck vertebrae and trachea can be caused by hard jerks on a slip collar. There are more humane collars, such as limited slip collars or head halters, that work well for training and are easier to use and harder to misuse than the choke chain type.

Pinch or Prong Collars

These collars are interlinking pieces of heavy steel wire bent so the ends of each link pinch vise-like into the skin on the dog's neck when the leash is pulled. This, of course, causes pain—how much pain depends on how heavy-handed the trainer is. Pinch collars are designed for use in training methods that teach the dog to avoid pain by obeying commands before the handler punishes him with the prongs.

Years ago prong collars were used only on dogs being trained for attack work. Now, they have found their way into the hands of pet owners, and, unfortunately, through both ignorance and meanness, are often used abusively. There are more humane ways to work with a dog (see below).

Limited Slip or "Combination" or "Martingale" Collars

These are very humane and effective for general wear and many types of training. Limited slip collars are easy to use and

The flat collar fastens with a nonslip buckle or clasp.

hard to misuse. They are usually made of flat nylon fabric, come in a variety of colors and patterns, and are durable, adjustable, and comfortable. These collars have an adjustable limited slip action that presses

This is a prong or pinch training collar.

more on the muscles around the neck than on the trachea. As with any slip-type collar, a dog should wear one only when supervised because it could get caught and trap him.

Head Halters

These are another very humane training tool. Used in conjunction with, or instead of, a collar, the halter works on the principles of leverage that give even small handlers an advantage over big dogs. Like a miniaturized horse halter, these have a band that goes around the muzzle but does not hold the mouth shut. The leash attaches to a ring on that band, so when the dog pulls, his head will be turned away from the direction he wants to go. The handler doesn't need to pull on the

The head halter is a gentle training tool.

leash to correct the dog, but merely stands still until the dog realizes he's not getting anywhere and lets some slack back into the leash. Used properly this is a very gentle and humane training tool that works extremely well on dogs that pull hard on leash. Even a young child could walk Buddy on a halter; of course, an adult should still supervise. This device gives the handler power steering without hurting the dog.

Most dogs object to head halters when they are first introduced, and try to rub or paw the band from around the muzzle. This is not because the halter is uncomfortable, but because the dog has grown used to dragging his handler and resents being controlled in any way. Most dogs will quickly get over this if you combine wearing the halter with nice treats, walks, companionship, and praise.

Some people do not like the look of the halter because it reminds them of a muzzle. It is not a muzzle at all, but sometimes a negative emotional reaction causes uninformed handlers to reject the use of this excellent humane training tool. To improve the look of, and public reaction to, the halter, sew or glue some colorful appliqués or embroidered trim over the noseband. This makes it very attractive and showy, which immediately changes most viewers' reactions from negative to positive. Head halters are used successfully by many dog owners and are recommended by many professional dog trainers.

Harnesses

Although most harnesses are built to allow the dog to pull as hard as he likes, special walking harnesses are made to prevent dogs from tugging at the lead. Some older styles of no-pull harnesses put pressure under the forelegs, making the dog uncomfortable when he pulls. The newer type of no-pull harness is designed with a leash attachment ring on the band that goes across the dog's chest. There are several styles of these front-attachment harnesses. They all work by steering the dog away from the direction he's pulling, much as a taut anchor line on a boat's bow will turn the bow around to face the anchor. The dog learns he must leave some slack in the leash if he wants to walk straight ahead. If a harness chafes or irritates the skin behind the dog's forelegs, it may be the wrong size or improperly adjusted. Discontinue use until the irritation clears up, and make sure it fits correctly before using it again.

Leashes

The leash is a control device and a communication tool that links Buddy to you when you are training or just out for a stroll. Sometimes you'll use your leash to restrain or correct, but it's also a telegraph line, conveying important information between you and Buddy.

A harness is for pulling, as when tracking.

Traffic Leads

These are about 2 feet (61 cm) long, so when the traffic lead is held by the handler, the dog must walk close beside him or her. Handlers whose dogs are fairly reliable off lead sometimes use a traffic lead as a handle to grab when they need closer control.

A 6-foot (1.8-m) training lead allows the handler to keep the dog close or permit more freedom.

The retractable lead extends for more freedom and retracts for control.

how much slack you want in the leash between you and Buddy, then fold the rest neatly into your palm. Adjusting the length is simple—just play out what you want and close your fist on the rest. Avoid wrapping the leash around your hand; people have broken fingers doing that.

Drawback: Improper leash management; taking up slack by wrapping around the hand multiple times can injure the handler.

Drawbacks: Very short, not useful for general training.

Walking Leads

These are about 4 feet (1.2 m) long and are used when the dog will be heeling most of the time. One of these can serve as a grab handle when beginning off-leash training, as it can be held or dropped without interfering with the full-grown Lab's movement.

Drawback: Too short for most on-leash training work.

Training Leads

These are 6 feet (1.8 m) long. Held correctly, the leash is quite versatile, allowing the handler to keep the dog close or let him stroll freely. When heeling, decide

Retractable Leads

These leads are spring-loaded spools of cord or flat tape inside plastic cases with handles. As the dog pulls, the spool unwinds, giving him a longer leash. As he returns to the handler, the lead retracts.

Drawback: The way this operates teaches the dog to pull on the lead.

Long Lines

These are what the name says—long (10 to 50 feet, 3 to 15 m) lines. They can be of webbed fabric or lightweight 1/8- to 1/4-inch (3.2- to 6.4-mm) nylon cord. Long lines give the dog a sense of freedom, yet allow the handler to remind him, from a distance, to obey.

Drawback: It takes practice to avoid tangling long lines.

5 *Leadership and Mutual Respect*

What Is a Pack Leader?

Dogs are pack animals by nature. One or two confident, experienced adults (often a mated pair) lead the pack and make decisions for the well-being of the group. The pack leader protects the pack from outside aggressors and keeps order among the members to minimize fighting.

Along with the responsibilities of leadership also come benefits. The pack leader has first choice of the food and the comfortable resting spots and has the right to either keep those good things or share them at will.

You might wonder how this description of a dog pack pertains to how you should raise and train your Lab. A lot of people talk about being your dog's pack leader, and some insist we must act like dogs ourselves, dominating our dogs as another dog might, if we want our dogs to do as we say. Fortunately, this isn't true, as most humans aren't very convincing when they try to mimic canines.

The concepts of dominance and submission are frequently misunderstood, as

is the true nature of a pack leader. A good pack leader doesn't waste energy constantly forcing other pack members to act submissively. A good leader doesn't need to snap and snarl and shove others around to prove he's boss. That would only tire him out and create stress for the group. The status of a strong pack leader can be seen in the quiet confidence of his behavior, and that behavior inspires others to follow him. The pack's stability depends not only on wise and confident leadership, but also on willing cooperation and mutual respect.

But your Lab is *not* a wild dog living in a dog pack. He is part of your family. You protect him, provide for him, and teach him the good manners and cooperation skills he needs to get along well with humans. For Buddy to become the cooperative and trustworthy companion you want him to be, you'll need to do that, and as Buddy's leader and caregiver, that is your job. You are his leader, yes, but you are not a dog, you are a human being, and you'll be happy to know that you can teach Buddy everything he needs to learn without trying to pretend you're a dominant dog.

Reasons Not to Use Dominance Training

Harsh displays of physical dominance like grabbing a pup's neck scruff, flipping him onto his back, and holding him down, teaches by example that leaders use force and violence to get their way. It's scary for a pup to have this done by someone he trusts, and it can make him fear the person doing it. He may also start distrusting other people, and may shy away or try to defend himself when people reach for his collar or touch his head or neck. This can become a dangerous reaction, especially when children or guests innocently try to pet him.

A pup must learn to trust people and to calmly accept handling. This is important for everyone's safety, including that of the dog. Training and handling should be done gently and with respect for the dog.

Your actions teach Buddy how a grown-up leader acts. Violence begets violence, so don't model that behavior. If you bully your pup, he may learn to be a bully, just like you. Old-fashioned, forceful *alpha dominance training* does not set a positive example. Domination with physical force produces fear, not respect. A better way to teach good manners and reliable, nonviolent behavior is with *trust training.*

Trust Training

Teach Buddy to allow you to touch him all over his body, including his head, tail, paws, and belly. Do this calmly and gently, so your touch feels pleasant to him. If you find an area where he resists being touched, don't force the situation. Go back to the area you handled previously to remind him that your touch feels good. Then one short, gentle stroke at a time, revisit the sensitive spot, but don't overdo it. When a dog resists being touched in a particular area, there's sometimes a physical reason, so as you touch him, check gently for lumps, thorns, scabs, missing hair, or a noticeable difference in skin temperature. Gently handle Buddy's head. Stroke his ears, lips, and the area around his eyes. Touch his cheeks, brow, and neck. And when he's relaxed about having his topside handled, teach him to lie on his back and enjoy a gentle tummy rub.

Don't force him over, just gently stroke him until he relaxes, then carefully roll him as you continue to pet. When Buddy accepts this as a pleasant routine, have each family member sit beside you and stroke the dog softly while he lies on his back. Although this is a submissive posture, Buddy will learn to enjoy it because

> **Note:** Imagine the size Buddy will be at maturity, then magnify his puppy misbehaviors by that amount. Dogs grow very fast and habits that are cute now may be ugly in six months, as Buddy grows bigger and more powerful. Allowing or encouraging "cute" puppy misbehaviors is a bad mistake.

it feels good. This will teach him not to worry when people touch him.

Another facet of trust training is teaching Buddy not to guard his food or toys. Many dogs guard their food and possessions from other dogs; this is a natural behavior. You can teach Buddy that he doesn't need to guard his treasures from you. Start by splitting his meal in two and putting only half of it in his bowl. When he's finished eating the first half, say, "Thank you" or "Give," then pick it up and hand feed him about a tablespoon of the remaining food. Put the rest into the bowl and put it down for him to eat. After doing that for several meals say "Here you go," and put the second part of his meal in the bowl without picking it up when he finishes the first part. Do that for several meals, then add the second part while he's still eating the first. After he's comfortable with that, pull the bowl slightly toward you when adding the second portion. Progress to picking up his bowl to add the second portion. Buddy will soon become optimistic that when you reach for his bowl, you'll be adding food, and he'll soon look forward to these interruptions. When he's completely comfortable with you handling his bowl while he's eating, help each of your family members to do the same.

This strategy also works for teaching dogs to willingly give up toys and other items. Teach Buddy that when you take something away, you'll either give it right back, plus praise and sometimes a yummy treat, or you'll trade it for a different but equally enjoyable item. Buddy will learn to trust that you are fair and generous, and he won't think he needs to guard his treasures from you.

Family Members and Children

If your household consists of more than just you and Buddy, he will need to learn to be gentle, cooperative, and obedient with all members of your family. For this to happen, your whole family needs to understand and honor the rules you've set for Buddy. For example, if you're teaching Buddy to sit politely for greetings, but your teen or spouse encourages him to jump on them and wrestle when saying hello, that will confuse the dog and undermine the training you've done with him.

Hold a family meeting to talk about the "Buddy Rules." The best time to do this is before you get the dog or as soon as possible after he joins your family. Ask for input from all family members, including children, because people are usually more cooperative about keeping rules if they help design them. Be realistic

An adult should always supervise young children who are around dogs.

Encourage your pup to make friends with people, especially children. The first month with your Lab is an important bonding period.

can teach your children to help train Buddy by using treats as rewards. Dole out the treats to the trainer-child one by one or she may give the dog too large a reward. Make sure Buddy actually does what the child tells him before he gets the reward. Make it clear to children that they must not try to physically force Buddy to do what they say, and that if he won't listen to them, they should come to you for help.

Socialization

A dog is a social creature, and a good circle of friends will help him live a happy life. You, of course, are your dog's best friend, but Buddy also should know other people. To become trusting and well adjusted, a dog should be socialized around people and dogs to prevent an attitude of fear or aggression.

The happiest dog is the one with an owner-leader to adore, people friends and family to cuddle and play with, and canine pals to romp and wrestle with. Without good friends, even the sweetest-natured dog can become untrusting and antisocial. Avoid trouble by helping your dog form good friendships with people and dogs.

about your expectations for the dog's behavior. It will take time for him to learn all the rules, and he'll need patient training, gentle guidance, and family cooperation to succeed.

Most Labs enjoy children, but they view them more as pals than as leaders. Both kids and dogs tend to be impulsive at times, and their games can become overly rough. This can endanger both the children and the dog, so it's important to keep an eye on them and supervise their play. You

People Friends

Puppies are cute—no one can deny that. Most humans, even those intimidated by grown dogs, become putty in the paws of a pup. Women and children are not the only ones who succumb; "macho" men also coo baby talk to puppies.

> **Note:** It often increases the chaos of the situation if you try to carry a wiggling, nipping, thrashing pup to his pen or crate for a time-out. You may find it easier to administer the time-out by leaving the room yourself and closing the door or puppy gate behind you. Do this only if the area has been puppy-proofed, though.

Some of your friends may be eager to meet your new Lab. Wonderful! They'll be Buddy's extended family. But try to avoid having everyone show up at the same time. Buddy will do better if he can meet new friends individually or in groups of two or three, as pups can become overexcited and overwhelmed trying to meet too many new friends at once.

People are often more tolerant of a puppy nipping and jumping than they are once the dog attains some size. It is never too early to teach good manners, so start right away, while his misbehaviors seem almost cute.

A dog must be taught to act politely around people. Most Labradors are high-spirited, friendly, and athletic, which means that they need to learn to control their energy. With proper socialization and training, Labs can be one of the most stable breeds, but a full-grown untrained Lab is like an animated wrecking ball.

1. Teach Buddy to sit for greeting instead of allowing him to jump on you (see page 98). Have family members and friends do the same. A pup that learns this polite greeting will not form the habit of jumping up.

2. Teach Buddy not to chew on hands or tug on clothes by never allowing him to do this, even as a very young pup. When he starts nibbling on you, say "*Ow!*" in a stern voice, and freeze for a moment. Don't pull away or the pup will try to catch your hand. If he stops biting when he hears "*Ow!*" gently pet him and praise.

   If Buddy doesn't seem to be able to stop himself from chewing on you while you pet him, give him a toy to keep his mouth busy. If he drops the toy and grabs your hand again, stop petting him or playing, drop the toy, then turn your back on him and walk away. Ignore the pup for about 20 seconds to give him a chance to realize his playmate has quit the game. Then call him to you with a calm and kindly voice and give him a chance to be a gentle pup. If he resumes his bitey game, give him a five-minute time-out.

Dog Friends

Most modern dog owners are aware of the danger of communicable puppy diseases. A pup receives temporary immunity from the mother, which protects him until his own immune system matures and forms antibodies.

Pups usually start their immunization series at six or seven weeks and receive booster shots every few weeks to minimize risk of disease between the time maternal antibodies fade and the pup's immune system kicks in. Young pups may

Puppies need social experience with other dogs.

or may not be adequately protected, depending on the development of their immune systems, so sensible owners avoid exposing them to illness.

Some take this caution to extremes, isolating pups from the outside world until completing immunization. This isolation is well-intentioned but ill-advised: Pups need early experience with dogs and humans to become confident in social situations. Take precautions, but do socialize your pup.

Puppy Kindergarten

One of the best ways to help Buddy gain confidence and social skills is to enroll him in puppy kindergarten. Many trainers give puppy classes for dogs as young as seven or eight weeks. Puppy kindergarten classes should be taught by gentle methods using treats, toys, and games to build obedience and social skills. Early training around other dogs and their owners will give him a good start.

6 Health

Labrador Retrievers are powerful and sturdy dogs. Their average life span is about 10 or 12, but some Labs live years beyond that. With regular health care, both length and quality will be added to Buddy's life.

Immunization

Complete immunization may be the best health insurance you can provide for your pup. It is important to follow the vaccination schedule your veterinarian recommends. If Buddy is due for a booster on a certain date, make sure he receives it; a delay can leave him unprotected.

A newborn pup receives a dose of his mother's own antibodies. This confers a temporary protection against diseases. For several weeks to several months, those antibodies protect a pup, but when his own immune system matures, those maternal antibodies fade away.

Most veterinarians recommend vaccinating pups every few weeks from two to four months to reduce the chances of disease, although some advise less frequent vaccination. By four months the immune system is normally active, so one more set of shots is usually given at that age, just to be certain the pup is protected.

Environment— Housing, Diet, Grooming, Exercise

Buddy's environment will affect his health and longevity. Most Labs have sturdy bodies and optimistic attitudes, allowing them to weather life's hardships without falling apart, but even the hardiest Lab will stay healthier and live longer when receiving quality care. Buddy should thrive if you provide him with comfortable housing, nutritious food, sufficient exercise, and a clean body.

Housing

Dogs that live indoors with their human family often live longer and healthier lives than backyard kennel dogs. One reason for this is that a house dog lives more closely with his owner, who may notice signs of illness or injury sooner than owners of outside dogs. Another reason is that house dogs are not continually assaulted by weather changes and extremes. A Lab is a fairly durable creature, but clean, comfortable quarters can improve his health and the quality of his life.

Regular veterinary care throughout life is important for health.

excellent commercial dog foods. There are also several good books available with tested recipes for homemade rations, both cooked and raw.

Whether you choose to feed a high-quality commercial ration or cook fresh meals for him, be sure the diet is balanced and nutritionally complete. All body systems must be properly nourished to function efficiently, so nutrients must be consumed in balanced amounts. Too much or too little of any component can be harmful. A healthy, well-nourished Lab has a glossy coat, sparkling eyes, abundant energy, an optimistic attitude, and only a mild odor.

If Buddy is an outside dog, you must provide him with adequate shelter from weather. This means good shade in summer and a well-insulated and properly ventilated, weather-proof doghouse year-round. Be sure the doghouse blocks out drafts, rain, and snow. In bad weather check daily for leaks or dampness from condensation. A wet doghouse will not keep a dog warm.

Diet

Buddy's diet is another important factor related to health and longevity. We are fortunate today to have a wide choice of

Grooming

Grooming is preventive health maintenance for your dog; be sure you don't neglect him just because Labs are an easy-care breed. At minimum, Buddy should receive weekly brushing and a full body examination. If you let him romp in fields or forests, always check him afterwards for burrs, thorns, fleas, and ticks. Feet should be checked daily for thorns or cuts, and toenails should be trimmed every one to three weeks.

Ears: A Lab's ear leathers can trap water and debris inside, predisposing him to fungal and bacterial infections. Check ears daily for irritation or dampness, especially after a swim or a romp in the field. Thoroughly dry inside Buddy's ears after swimming or baths, then shake in a dash of athlete's foot powder. (Do not pack it in; just a shake will do.) Ears kept dry and clean should stay healthy.

A weekly brushing will keep your Lab's skin and coat healthy.

To clean Buddy's ears, wrap gauze or tissue around your finger and gently wipe the inner surfaces clean of matter. Don't make any "packing" motions with *anything* in Buddy's ears and *never* probe inside the ear canal with anything, including cotton swabs, as you may damage Buddy's hearing.

Nail care: Nails should be short for best foot health. Overgrown nails can cause sore, deformed feet and painful injuries. Some Labs exercise enough (or dig enough holes) to wear down their own nails, but most need their nails trimmed once or twice a month. This is something you can do as part of Buddy's regular grooming routine. Teach Buddy to accept paw handling first; then nail trimming will be easier.

There are two basic types of nail trimmers: the scissors type with two opposed cutting blades, and the "guillotine" type with one sliding blade. Either will work,

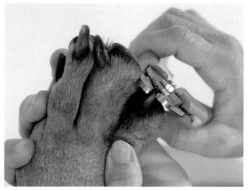

Nails should be trimmed at least once a month. When trimming, be careful not to cut off too much.

43

so which type you use is a matter of personal preference. The scissors type seems to hold up a bit better on dogs that have large or extra-hard nails.

Take care not to cut too deeply, as each toenail has a blood supply and nerves protected by the hard outer nail. If Buddy has light-colored nails, you can see a pinkish area inside, which is living tissue (the "quick"). Avoid cutting into that because it will hurt and may bleed. Trim off only a little slice at a time until you feel comfortable with this process. You can always cut off a little more if you take too little, but you can't put it back if you take too much. If you do nick the quick, don't panic. Apply firm pressure to the end of the nail with a tissue for about one minute, or until the bleeding stops. Deeper cuts may

require the application of a styptic powder, available at pet stores. Have this product on hand *before* you start.

Hold one paw gently but firmly, with Buddy's leg in a comfortable position. Steady the toe that you're working on between thumb and fingers while you trim. Place the blade where you intend to cut, double-check that it's not too deep, then squeeze the handles. Give Buddy a calm praise and treat break after every few nails so he will have something pleasant to look forward to when you trim.

Another useful tool for nail trimming is the electric or battery-powered rotary nail grinder. This handheld tool trims the dog's nails with a rapidly rotating cylinder of emery cloth. With a grinder you can quickly shorten nails and smooth their edges and there's very little risk of nicking the blood vessel. Left too long on one nail, the grinder can cause uncomfortable heat from friction. Solve this by grinding each nail in turn for only a few seconds at a time, repeating as many times as necessary to shorten them to the desired length.

Eye care: After a day in the field, be sure to check Buddy's eyelids for seeds or bits of dirt. Face the dog, holding his head between your hands. With one finger, gently pull down Buddy's lower eyelid and peek in, then raise his upper eyelid and check up there too. It should be pinkish, not bright red. Redness indicates inflammation that should be checked by a veterinarian if it persists.

Dirt and other small foreign objects can be removed from the eye by gently washing with large amounts of sterile saline eyewash (from the drugstore). If eyewash

An occasional bath will keep your Lab clean.

is not available, tap water can be used. If an object cannot be removed by gentle rinsing, the dog should receive immediate veterinary care.

Teeth care: Plaque can build up on a dog's teeth, causing gum disease, tooth loss, and harmful generalized infection. Regular teeth cleaning can prevent this. You can brush Buddy's teeth with a soft toothbrush and use toothpaste made especially for dogs. Dogs are not able to spit out toothpaste, so never use human toothpaste with Buddy, as it contains ingredients such as fluoride that should not be swallowed. Many human types of toothpaste also contain the sweetener xylitol, which is harmless to humans but can cause fatal poisoning in dogs. You can also wrap a piece of cotton gauze around your finger and rub the teeth instead of using a brush. Be sure to clean both the inner and outer surfaces of the teeth. Pay special attention to the back molars because that is where food tends to accumulate.

Dogs differ in the rate that plaque builds up on their teeth. Some dogs keep their teeth shiny white just by chewing. Others need frequent brushing, plus an annual tooth scaling done by the veterinarian. Ask your veterinarian for advice about your dog.

Exercise

Regular exercise is perhaps the most enjoyable component of health care. A healthy Lab has abundant energy that he must release through exercise. Without daily exercise Labs tend to become either rowdy or obese. Energy that is not released

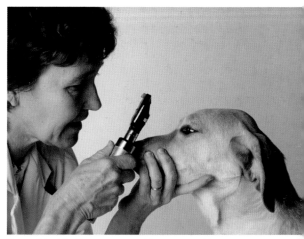

If an object in the eye cannot be removed by gentle rinsing, seek immediate veterinary attention.

through appropriate exercise leads to behavior problems such as barking, digging, and boundary aggression. Obesity makes a dog uncomfortable, reduces his desire to exercise, and may steal years from his life. Regular workouts and a balanced diet will extend Buddy's prime years.

Teaching Your Lab to Accept Health Care

Well-meaning owners sometimes avoid grooming and health care procedures that a dog does not appear to enjoy. This is a big mistake. Ignoring behavioral or medical problems in their early stages guarantees bigger problems later. Train Buddy to allow handling all over his body so you can take better care of him.

Massage for Health

Whole-body examination sometimes be a struggle when you first begin training, but dogs of any age can learn to accept handling and health care if it's a pleasant experience. You can make health care easier by teaching Buddy to enjoy a relaxing massage. The massage described below should be done slowly and should take about ten to fifteen minutes. Breathe deeply and evenly while you work on Buddy.

■ Begin at Buddy's neck with your fingertips in the groove at each side where his neck joins his shoulder, just below his collar.
■ Slowly slide the skin back and forth and in small circles, until the muscles underneath begin to soften. Don't press too hard or move too fast or you'll excite Buddy instead of relax him.
■ After the neck muscles have softened, slide the skin in circles up the neck, until you reach the groove where the ears join the back of the head. Gently slide the skin in small circles there, then massage the edge of the ears, all the way around, to the soft skin where the ear joins the top of the head.
■ Stroke from Buddy's nose up the bridge of his muzzle, then his forehead, to the bump at the back of the head. Do this several times with long, slow strokes, then slide your fingers down to the big, flat cheek muscles and move the skin in smooth circles. Many dogs relax noticeably when you do this and some will yawn to release stored tension.
■ Return to the neck/shoulder groove where you started. Work skin circles there until the muscles are relaxed, then massage the shoulders and down the front legs. Pay attention to leg joints; they may be sensitive.
■ Gently hold a front paw, as if you are holding hands. At first, do not massage; just stroke the paw gently until Buddy is relaxed. With a very sensitive dog this may be all you can do the first session. Touch each toe individually and buff the nail with your thumb, then stroke from shoulder to paw several times.
■ Return again to the neck/shoulder groove and check that it's still relaxed, then bridge the spine, with your thumb

Massage is good for health, relaxation, and bonding.

on one side and fingers on the other. Do not press on the spine bones, only the muscle on either side. Gently press and release once for each vertebra from neck to tail, then encircle the tail with your hand and gently stroke from base to tip.

■ Return again to the neck groove, then "comb" the ribs with your fingertips from spine to sternum. If you cannot feel individual ribs, Buddy may be overweight—check with your veterinarian. Follow the contour of the rib cage with your fingertips between ribs. Be gentle—this tickles if you press hard. Afterward, gently stroke the belly several times.

■ Return to the neck, check for tension, then stroke the length of the dog to his hip and place your palm over the hip joint. Moving slowly, gently circle the skin over the joint, then work down each hind leg, holding and massaging the rear paws and buffing each toenail with your thumb.

■ Last, with long, light strokes, sweep your fingertips several times from Buddy's head to his tail and down each leg. Finish by stroking his head and neck several times.

Taking Medicine

You can easily teach Buddy to swallow pills by hiding them in some tasty food, but if you've tried that and Buddy licked off the food and spat out the hidden pill, then try the following method.

The best foods for hiding pills stick to the medication until it goes down: soft cheese, butter, liverwurst, or a bite-sized peanut butter-and-pill sandwich. Some Labs are so food-crazy that even plain bread will work.

Here is the trick to use for a dog that licks off the tasty covering and spits out the pill: Don't make just one food ball and hide a pill inside; make three balls. The first is a blank—no pill. Give this to Buddy, and let him take his time and discover there's no hidden medicine. Then give him the second food ball—this one has the pill in it. As soon as Buddy takes the medicated food from your hand, offer the third ball—another blank. Most Labs will greedily gulp down the medicine and grab the next offer.

Mild-tasting liquid medicine may be mixed with a food Buddy craves—perhaps a bit of your own dinner. Make it super-appealing, because you'll have only one chance. If a dog rejects liquid medicine mixed with food, the dosage is wasted, unlike spit-out pills, which can be picked up off the floor and readministered.

Medicine can be given the no-cooperation way, if necessary:

For liquids, pull Buddy's lip corner out to form a pocket and pour the dose in. Then—quickly!—put your hand under his jaw to keep his mouth shut and his chin up. Stroke down his throat gently until he

> **Note:** Before hiding medicine in food, check with your veterinarian to be sure it does not have to be taken while fasting.

The veterinarian is truly one of your dog's best friends. The trouble is, Buddy may not realize that.

swallows *twice.* If you let go too soon, he'll shake his head, flinging medicine all over.

For pills, open his mouth and place the pill at the back of his tongue, close his mouth, lift his chin, and stroke his throat downward gently until he swallows *twice.*

Becoming Friends with the Veterinarian

The veterinarian is truly one of your dog's best friends. The trouble is, Buddy may not realize that. If he has been to the veterinary clinic only for vaccinations and opera-

tions, he's not likely to form pleasant associations with the place, which leads to a negative attitude. This may manifest itself in fear or aggression and make Buddy difficult to examine and treat.

This problem can be prevented by visiting the clinic occasionally just to check Buddy's weight and chat a moment with the receptionist. If she would pet and speak to Buddy, that would probably help. If the doctor could also do so, that's even better. If the clinic is busy when you drop in, do not bother the staff, but ask if there is a time they might be less rushed. If the clinic is always so busy that staff cannot talk to or pet waiting dogs, perhaps they're not interested enough in the emotional well-being of the animals they serve, and perhaps you can find a veterinarian who is.

7 *Motivating Your Labrador*

How Motivation Works

Motivation is the impulse that stirs a dog (or human) into action. When an action results in a consequence Buddy likes (reward), he will want to repeat it in the future. But if the action's consequence is undesirable to Buddy (punishment), his motivation to repeat that behavior in the future will decrease.

Dogs, like the rest of us, are motivated by the desire to attain certain objects or outcomes. Dogs desire companionship and approval, enjoy playing entertaining games, and like to satisfy taste cravings. To motivate Buddy to do what you want him to do, teach him that, in return for his cooperation, you'll give him the things he wants. Select rewards from among his favorite foods, games, toys, and cuddles. It's best to use a variety of rewards to prevent him from becoming bored. Regardless of how much a dog likes one particular treat or game, a reward will lose value if it becomes too commonplace.

Using Rewards

When Buddy earns rewards for doing certain actions, he'll be motivated to do those again and again, so make sure you reward him for actions you approve of and avoid accidentally rewarding for behavior he shouldn't do.

Rewards work best if you control the supply. For example, most Labs enjoy eating, so food can be a useful training reward. However, if you leave a never-empty bowl of kibble for Buddy to snack from anytime he likes, food will lose some of its value as a training reward. Instead of leaving food available all day long, feed Buddy scheduled meals, then remove any leftovers after twenty minutes. Making between-meal food available only from you will increase its value for Buddy and make it a more powerful reward.

Food is a training reward that will motivate most Labs, but food is not the only reward you can use. What else does Buddy like? What are his favorite playthings? Toys, balls, pinecones, empty bath-tissue tubes? What does he enjoy doing? Going for walks, swimming, fetching? What does he like you to do for him? Stroke his brow, rub his ears, and scratch his rump? Make a list of Buddy's Fifteen Favorite Things. Be specific. Don't just write "food"; itemize Buddy's favorite treats—cheese, hot dogs, pizza crusts, and so on. Do the same with toys—tennis ball, tug-rope, squeaky bone, and so on. Any number of items on this list can potentially be used as training rewards. The more highly Buddy values the item, the more powerful a reward it will be.

Treat Rewards

Food is a strong incentive for most Labs. Occasionally, a Lab may be picky about what he eats, but most Labs are eager for food, even when not truly hungry; therefore, food can be used as a lure to elicit behavior, as a prize to reward obedience, or both. Using treats as part of the train-

Dogs enjoy being part of a human-family pack.

ing program can have a positive effect on Buddy's learning curve.

A food lure is a handheld treat that the dog follows to the commanded position. Buddy learns to watch the hand moving the lure, which teaches the hand signals specific to each command. With practice, Buddy will learn to obey spoken or signaled commands equally well.

A food reward is a treat given to the dog after he obeys, but food alone is not a sufficient reward. A dog that will work only for food rewards is not truly obedient; therefore, use praise just before giving a treat reward to enhance the value of both. Treats are useful to capture a dog's attention and motivate him to learn, but over time you should phase out the treats so Buddy will work for praise (see page 60 to learn how to use food in training).

When using treats as training rewards, remember that they count as part of Buddy's food intake. Your Lab will put on excess weight if he consumes more calories daily than he uses to fuel his physical activity, so use healthful treats no larger than a bean and cut back a little on the size of regular meals. Most Labs enjoy earning any kind of treat, and you may find Buddy will work happily for bits of his regular food as training rewards. Other healthful treats might include bean-sized bits of cheese or meat, thin slices of apple or carrot, or individual pieces of unsweetened breakfast cereal.

Praise

Your happy, pleased voice is music to your dog's ears. Praise is a strong reward on its

Petting is often a good reward.

own and also magnifies other rewards. Praise first to mark the behavior you liked, then give the other reward. Praise will signal to Buddy that he has done right and inform him there may be more rewards coming. This motivates his attention. As Buddy masters his lessons, gradually wean him away from treats by switching from treat-plus-praise to praise alone, praise with petting, or praise with release to an activity Buddy enjoys.

Well-timed, sincere praise will strengthen Buddy's desire to learn and obey. Praise represents your approval of Buddy's deeds. This makes him feel secure. When his leader is pleased, a dog basks in that warm, protective glow.

Voice Tone

The tone of your praise can help motivate your dog. Praise with a soft voice to calm and reassure Buddy that all is well. Use a happy, excited voice to energize him and encourage greater attempts. Be specific with praise. Use a short phrase that includes both praise and the command Buddy has obeyed, as in *"Good sit!"* This lets him know exactly what pleases you about his behavior. Saying just *"Good dog"* or *"Good Buddy"* tells him you're pleased, but gives no indication of what he has done to please you. A praise phrase tells a dog exactly what you liked about his behavior and, at the same time, it warns him not to try random or unapproved actions.

Physical Touch

When a litter of pups naps, they'll sometimes stack themselves two and three deep in a pile. This is for not only physical warmth, but also security and friendship. Dogs crave touch, and stroking and petting them as a reward helps satisfy that natural desire.

Different types of touch affect dogs in different ways. Touch can reward or punish, stimulate or calm. You can help balance Buddy's energy by touching him in certain ways. To soothe him, pet slowly, with long strokes. Pat more quickly to excite a bored dog. To calm a worried or anxious dog, pat with a slow, loose-wristed thumping along his shoulder or ribs, as if you were trying to puff dry dust out of his fur. As you discover Buddy's favorite strokes you will find more ways to soothe his nerves, stimulate his energy, and reward good behavior.

Some Labs think play is the best reward.

Hunting and Chasing

Most dogs have a prey drive, the natural desire to chase moving objects. Labs are no exception, as this breed has a strong hunting background. A moving object in a dog's visual range may distract him from a lesson, but movement can also motivate a dog to greater achievement. The key is in how the handler uses it.

Fast motions excite a dog and entice him to spring into action. Slower movements can hold his interest and build concentration. Abrupt stop-and-go motions may be interpreted as an invitation to play.

If a movement includes touch, it will heighten a dog's excitement, sometimes to extremes, causing wiggliness and loss of attention. Fast movement plus touch may overstimulate some dogs to nip or bite. The canine impulse is to grab whatever moves close, so be sensitive with movement and touch and avoid overstimulating your dog.

Play

Dogs learn and practice life skills by playing games. Most natural dog games are based on survival needs and strengthen the players mentally and physically. At about four or five weeks of age, puppies play pre-games like Catch Mama's Tail and Nip Sibling's Nose. As they gain strength and coordination a rank order forms among the littermates. Baby games progress to rowdy ones as puppies play-fight with each other, and play-kill their toys. Play is fun but it's not trivial. Muscle, wit, and reflexes are honed sharp by games to be ready for action when real life demands.

When working or playing with Buddy, watch for clues that tell what motivates him, then use that to shape his behavior. Hold your dog's interest with what he enjoys. Include what he likes best in training and Buddy will be motivated to learn anything you teach.

8 Communicating with Your Lab

Capturing and Holding Your Dog's Attention

Take a stroll with Buddy and watch how his ears, eyes, and nose catalog his surroundings. You'll note that Buddy logs many more sounds, sights, and scents than you'd notice on your own. You might also find that when your dog is interested in those other attractions, he pays little attention to you. Therein lies the problem. A dog that does not listen and obey when distracted places himself at risk. He may become lost or injured when he ignores his handler, so it's vital that you teach him to pay attention to you, regardless of what else may be happening around him. The trick to generating that kind of focus is to make yourself the most interesting attraction. This is a tall order. Capturing and holding your dog's attention will require consistent work, but the results will be worth the effort.

When first teaching Buddy a new skill, work in a fairly quiet area with as few distractions as possible. When he has successfully learned the new skill, try adding minor distractions to your surroundings, gradually adding more as Buddy's focus on you improves. Too many distractions at once will steal Buddy's attention and hinder his learning, so don't add more than he can tolerate without losing focus on the lesson.

Attention Training

To obey commands Buddy must first learn to pay attention when you speak to him. Handlers often make the mistake of repeating themselves. ("*Buddy! Hey, Buddy! Sit, boy. Sit. Sit. Sit.*") This tells the dog that he isn't really expected to listen because the more the handler repeats the commands, the less attention the dog pays to them. Some dogs learn to shut out the owner's echoing voice altogether. This is unpleasant for the owner and unsafe for the dog. If Buddy's response to command is slow or absent when distracted, it's time for attention training.

Attention training is not a contest of wills; it's easy and fun and forges a strong bond between dog and handler. Buddy learns that to get a reward he has to listen closely. A dog that pays attention to your voice is more likely to obey commands. To begin attention training, teach Buddy to look at you when you say his name.

1. First, say your dog's name when he is not looking at you. Speak clearly and don't repeat yourself.
2. If your dog looks at you, praise "*Good Buddy!*" and reward him with petting and a small treat. Then allow him to become interested in other things for a few minutes, then again say his name when he's not looking at you, and reward him immediately when he turns his attention to you.
3. If Buddy ignores your call, touch him lightly on the rear part of his body. When he turns around to see what's tickling him, smile, praise "*Good Buddy*," and give him a treat. Wait a while, then do it again.

Practice the attention training exercise about a dozen times a day. In three days or less Buddy should be looking at you immediately whenever you say his name.

Eye Contact

It is pleasant for dog and handler to exchange affectionate eye contact, but prolonged staring can make a dog uncomfortable because in dog language locked eyes signal aggression and a willingness to fight. A dog that does not wish to fight will avert his eyes from a direct stare. An aggressive dog, however, may attack.

To avoid problems, teach Buddy to hold eye contact with you. After you've achieved good name response with attention training, look into your dog's eyes for a moment just before giving the reward. Say "*Buddy, look at me,*" and hold a treat at your temple, next to your eye. Wait until Buddy offers a flicker of eye contact, then smile, praise, and give the reward. Hold his gaze a little longer each time before giving him the treat.

Next, without a treat in your hand, say his name. When he looks at you, point to your eye. Encourage Buddy to make eye contact and hold his gaze for a moment, then reward him with a treat from your pocket. This exercise builds attention and reduces the instinctive stress a dog feels with prolonged eye contact.

For best attention, encourage your Lab to make eye contact.

Hand Signals

You can use your hands to communicate with Buddy through both visual and auditory signals. Clapping or snapping your fingers will produce sounds that interrupt Buddy's activity and signal him to look at you. Once you have his attention, you can give him a hand signal. They are easier for most dogs to learn than verbal commands.

With hand signals alone you can command a dog to sit, lie down, stand, turn left or right, slow down, speed up, go out, come back, and more. Food lures are quite useful for teaching hand signals. While watching a treat lure, Buddy learns to pay attention to the movement of your hand (see page 60 for how to use a food lure).

Understanding Dog Language

Dogs communicate with a natural language of body postures and vocalizations that can send messages over quite a distance. Attention-getting vocalizations such as barking and growling are augmented and fine-tuned with facial expressions and body movements. Head and tail carriage and muscle tension send signals of rank and intent.

Body Posture

To express dominance a dog will make himself appear as large and formidable as possible. Dogs in a dominance contest rise up on their toes, trying to position their head and neck higher than those of their opponent. Surprisingly, the most dominant dog is not always the largest. A convincing pose rates higher in a rank display than body bulk. The dominant pose includes a forward-facing stance, raised head, stiff posture, and a high tail. The dog that maintains the most convincing stance is recognized as the top dog. Ritualized posturing often allows dominance to be expressed without the need for an actual fight.

A dog's rank and intent can be read in his head inclination:

- A high head, facing forward, communicates bold self-confidence.
- Head cocked to the side signals curiosity.
- A low head with eyes averted, and body angled slightly to the side communicates submission or nonaggression. Don't be fooled by a low head if the dog is making direct eye contact; that is a defensive stance warning of self-protective aggression.

Dogs also communicate intent by their direction of approach. Approaching a strange dog or person in a direct straight path signals dominance. A low-ranking dog normally approaches his superiors along a slightly curved path. A dog that bends his body sideways and wags his tail low as he approaches is offering appeasement.

Your own body language is important to dogs. Your posture may noticeably affect the way Buddy responds. Stand tall and appear confident for best results. You don't need to be a six-footer to inspire leadership; just have a confident pose.

Your body language is important to dogs.
Stand tall and appear confident.

Buddy may still like you as a pal, but won't respect you as a leader and will tend to ignore your commands.

If Buddy has a soft temperament or is on the submissive side, it's still best to use the erect posture. A confident stance gives a nervous or timid dog the impression you're a capable leader. That will help him feel safe so he can relax and cooperate, rather than worrying about protecting himself.

Calming Signals

Dogs send calming signals to each other to defuse aggression. To communicate peaceful intent, a dog might turn his head and yawn, or he might reduce potential conflict by busying himself scratching an imaginary flea.

If your dog is anxious, you can reassure him by sending canine calming signals. Turn your head to the side and yawn. Slouch a little and rub your elbow or neck. Sit down. Eat a snack. These actions have a calming influence and reduce anxiety in dogs.

Facial and Eye Expressions

Facial expression is a strong communication tool for both dogs and humans. Tiny muscles around lips, cheeks, eyes, and ears create subtle changes in expression that are important for clear communication; slight differences in facial expression send significantly different messages. An aggressive dog might lift his lips, exposing teeth bared in warning, but a show of

Throw your shoulders back and hold your head high. Look like a leader; the straighter you stand, the greater authority you'll communicate. When Buddy sees by your posture that you feel confident, he will believe you know what you're doing and will be more willing to cooperate with you.

A slouched posture conveys lack of confidence, tempting a bossy dog to treat you as an underling. If you lack authority, teeth, combined with low posture and a wagging tail, conveys submission. To avoid misinterpreting facial subtleties, observe postural clues as well.

"The eyes are the windows of the soul" is an accurate old saying, for eye expression can convey an individual's inner emotional state. By looking into Buddy's eyes you can discern his mood; if he is happy, sad, angry, loving, or confused, his eyes will tell. Fear and worry cause muscles around the eyes to tense. A worried dog continually shifts his gaze, as if expecting the approach of trouble, whereas the eyes of a confident dog express positive interest in surroundings but not worry.

Watch the eyes for signals, but don't stare, especially with an aggressive dog or one whose temperament you're not sure of. A direct stare calls for direct action—either dominant or submissive. Staring at an aggressive dog may trigger an attack, and prolonged eye contact with a timid dog may produce submissive urination.

You may safely gaze into your own dog's eyes if you've taken the time to do the attention training and eye contact exercises described earlier. Teach Buddy that eye contact can be a nonthreatening expression of affection or interest. Acceptance of prolonged eye contact can prevent dangerous miscommunication between Buddy and unwitting strangers who stare.

Touch

Touch is important to dogs when communicating and bonding with pack members. Nuzzling, licking, and gentle body contact are signs of affection that a pup first learns from his dam. Licking is a friendly gesture usually initiated by a submissive dog toward a dominant one. Dogs offer similar affectionate contact to people they love. Excessive licking is bossy, however, rather than sweetly affectionate. Overly effusive displays of affection should be controlled by teaching the dog to sit politely for greeting and to hold a toy in his mouth instead of licking.

Bumping with the nose is another bossy habit that may begin as a playful gesture. Bumping is used to get a game started with a peer or to trigger flight in a prey animal. Nose nudging is often accompanied by pawing or mouthing. These impolite attempts to manipulate people should not be permitted.

The way you pet Buddy can affect his energy level and mood. Your touch can communicate calming or exciting messages, depending on how you move your hands. Slow strokes have a relaxing effect, but quick patting or rubbing will invigorate him. To steady an anxious dog, pat his shoulder or side with a slow, thumping rhythm, keeping your hand and wrist very relaxed.

Vocal Sounds

Vocalization is important in canine communication. Although dogs do not use words, there are meanings behind their sounds. A high, loud voice is exciting; a low, soft voice relaxes and reassures. To settle Buddy, use a quiet voice. To communicate authority, use a low, clipped voice. High-pitched tones sound immature and

Both handler and dog are calm and relaxed.

for a favor, perhaps to be let in, or for someone to come romp with him.

Various breath sounds, though subtle, are another part of a dog's "spoken" language.

- Nervousness or fear is signaled by fast, shallow panting with moments of breath holding. An anxious dog, intermittently holding his breath, is preparing for fight or flight and you should avoid startling him.
- Quick panting, more audible on the exhale than the inhale, signifies playful intent.
- Fast panting, accompanied by frequent swallowing, may be a breath-catching pause in play or, accompanied by a tense facial expression, may indicate anxiety.

Growling is often a response to perceived danger, but not every growl carries a threat. A quiet growl with a soft rise at the end is a play sound often heard during competitive games, such as tug. The play growl carries an entirely different meaning than the rumbling growl of aggression. Body posture and facial expression will help you determine whether a growl is playful or serious.

submissive, so keep your voice at the low end of your normal range if you want him to take you seriously.

Barking is usually done to get attention. When Buddy barks, note which direction he's facing. Facing away from you, he may be noting and warning trespassers. Facing you, he's probably asking

Communication is a two-way street. Buddy must learn to listen to you, of course, but you'll need to understand him too. Knowing the dog language of posture, expression, and tone will help you understand what Buddy is trying to say and make you a more efficient trainer.

9 Commands— A Basic Vocabulary

Dogs and Language

The average dog's ability to learn specific words is remarkable, considering his own language uses postures, gestures, and vocal tones, not words. Numerous owners report dogs responding to more than 50 words or phrases and many admit they resort to spelling words such as "cookie" or "biscuit" or "walk" in the presence of canine eavesdroppers. Keep a list of the words Buddy responds to; you may be amazed at his vocabulary.

Most of the words a dog needs to know are either nouns or verbs. Nouns are things that dogs can eat or play with, such as "bone" or "ball." Verbs are actions that dogs can do, such as "sit" or "fetch." While learning commands Buddy will exercise his body and mind as the commands translate his high energy into controllable and praiseworthy behavior.

Health Check

Before starting Buddy in a rigorous training program for obedience, field work, Agility, or other athletic activity, have him thoroughly examined by the veterinarian. Congenital conformation faults may cause a dog discomfort and hardship in training. A Lab with vision problems may be unable to respond to a hand signal and one with impaired hearing may not heed a spoken command. A dog with joint problems might disobey a command to take an ordinary, but painful for him, position.

Do not assume slowness or refusal is intentional naughtiness. Let your veterinarian determine if a persistent or peculiar misbehavior has a physical cause. Buddy may be trying to tell you that something is wrong with his body.

Positive Obedience Training

Positive, reward-based techniques are best for teaching commands. The handler's job is to help the dog understand what is required and motivate him to act. As discussed in the previous chapter, dogs learn quickest when obedience earns an enjoyable reward, such as praise, petting, food, and play. Use the rewards in various combinations to maintain Buddy's interest in lessons. Vary the order of commands when practicing obedience work. Throw in a trick or two or an Agility obstacle. Keeping Buddy guessing at what the next activity will be can heighten interest and motivate him to pay closer attention.

Using Food Lures

Food is an excellent motivation for Labs because it piques their interest and makes learning more fun. Tidbit lures used in training focus a dog on the handler's hand, lure his body into completing the task, and reward his cooperation. With food lures, puppies as young as six weeks can be taught to come, sit, and lie down on command.

To use a food lure, show it to Buddy, then move it where you want his nose to be. If you move the lure skillfully, he will simply follow the treat into the position you indicate.

Following a lure helps the dog learn to watch the trainer's hand signal. Pairing verbal commands with hand signals teaches the dog to follow either voice or silent signal directions. Always praise just before you reward Buddy with a treat. The praise phrase ("*Good sit!*" for example) both marks the behavior and rewards it, because your dog will enjoy hearing your pleased tone. Eventually, the lure is phased out, then the treat reward too, so the dog will work for praise alone. Once in a while, just out of the blue, give a treat reward for obedience; it will make Buddy want to work harder.

The instructions that follow include both lure/reward and gentle physical positioning techniques for teaching commands. It's best to start off with the lure method when initially teaching what a command means. Use physical positioning in conjunction with lures when working with a rowdy or willful dog. Gentle physical positioning can also be used to correct an already trained dog that decides to ignore a command.

Walking on Leash

It's enjoyable to walk a dog that doesn't pull on the leash, but this blissful state is attained only through training. Most young pups naturally pull when on leash, but you can introduce them to better leash manners using praise, lures, and games. Rowdy adolescents and adults may require more persistence, but they can also be trained by rewarding their cooperation and correcting them using their own resistance.

Informal Walking

When exercising Buddy you may wish to allow a longer leash than you use for the formal *heel* position (see page 62). Use the *walk* command for this.

1. Attach a 6-foot (1.8-m) lead to Buddy's collar, command "*Walk,*" and start off. He may or may not follow. If he does, praise "*Good walk!*"
2. If he balks instead of follows, be patient. Do not drag a puppy that balks; it doesn't really help and might scare him badly. Just stand with your back to him with the leash loose and drop a few treats where he can see them. As he walks over to get the treats, keep the leash loose and just follow.

Some pups stage prolonged strikes; if so, just stand with your back to the pup until he gets bored with his protest. This should take only a few minutes, as most pups have a short attention span. Sometimes it helps to just pick up and carry the puppy several steps, then set him gently on his feet and keep on walking. If you act like you assume little Buddy will follow you, he very likely will.

If Buddy is big and rowdy, he might dash to the end of his leash, trying to tow you along. Be prepared. Hold your leash firmly against your midsection with both hands. Remember, Labs are strong.

When Buddy starts to pull, stand still and become a tree. Stand with your feet shoulder-width apart, and stare at a distant point just above eye level. This will cause most dogs, after a brief period of bored annoyance, to settle down.

If Buddy continues to pull while you stand firm, begin slowly backing away. It may take several steps before Buddy realizes he is losing ground by continuing to pull. Then he will turn around to check on what "your problem" might be. When he looks, praise him. Sometimes give a treat. Wait a moment to see if he resumes pulling. If he does not, then start walking forward again. Whenever Buddy pulls, stop and become a tree.

When Buddy settles, say "*Walk*," and start forward again. When Buddy is paying attention and not pulling, occasionally praise him happily—"*Good walk!*"—and sometimes give a treat.

Wait

Wait means "stop moving forward," but does not require the dog to take a particular position. This command can be taught in conjunction with *walk*.

Wait is a very useful command.

While walking, suddenly freeze, saying with a note of urgency "*Wait!*" Buddy will probably stop, as he would if another dog barked then froze. Praise "*Good wait!*," go to Buddy, pet him, and hold his collar. Give a treat and praise again "*Good wait!*" Then start out with *walk.*

Practice at street crossings, before passing through gates or doorways, and occasionally for no reason at all. Once Buddy learns *wait* while on leash, practice off lead as well. This is a very useful command.

Heel *and Automatic* Sit *(Formal Walking)*

With *heel* the dog's position is beside your left leg, close enough to be touched, but not in physical contact with you. When you stop, the dog is to sit beside you. You can teach this command to a dog of any age by luring him into position and rewarding with treats.

1. Hold your leash in your right hand and a treat in your left.
2. Say "*Heel*," and start to walk. Give Buddy a treat if he follows.
3. Hold the treat where you want Buddy's nose to be. His neck should be even with your leg. If he lags, move the treat forward to speed him up. If he forges ahead, move the treat back, or change direction. Occasionally stop and have Buddy sit at your left.
4. When Buddy is *heeling* well, following the lure, start holding it closer to your body. Later, when *heeling* is reliable, keep your treats in a pocket or pouch, occasionally giving one for quality work.

The Formal Recall

In the formal recall, you leave the dog on a *sit-stay*, walk away, turn to face him, wait a moment, and call your dog. The dog comes and sits close in front, facing you, then moves into *heel* position at your left when commanded.

Finish *to* Heel

The move to *heel* is called the *finish* and looks great when done well. Commands

At *heel* the dog is close beside the handler's left leg.

often used for this move are "*Heel*," "*Finish*," or "*Swing*." It doesn't really matter what command you choose; Buddy will learn whichever one you teach him. Most dogs readily learn to *finish* when lured with treats.

There are a couple of ways to *finish*. In one, the dog passes behind you from right to left ending in *heel* position at your left side. In the other, he pivots from in front of you to your left, into *heel* position. Either can be taught using treat lures, which also teach a hand signal for the move. Most dogs can learn both, stimulating their mental and physical skills and sharpening attention.

1. To teach Buddy to *finish* behind from right to left, stand facing him. Hold a treat in each hand.

2. Show Buddy the treat in your right hand and lure him behind you by moving your right hand behind you.
3. When your right hand is behind your back, attract Buddy's attention to the treat in your left hand. Bring your left hand forward, luring him into *heel* position, then lift the treat slightly so he sits, and reward him with praise and a treat.

The pivot to the left *finish* can be done with a leap and flourish or a simple, polite turn.

1. To teach this move, use a treat in your left hand to lure Buddy counterclockwise from in front of you to your left side so he ends up facing forward in *heel* position. It may help to walk forward a step or two at first to encourage your dog to follow the treat.
2. When Buddy reaches *heel* position, stop, then lift the treat, cueing for a *sit*.

Graduating to Off-leash Work

To prepare for off-leash work, remember to keep a loose leash when you teach *heeling* and other work. A constantly tight leash will make unclipping the lead seem like a cue for Buddy to ignore you. Keep your leash slack except when using it to communicate a message.

When Buddy is doing well on leash, switch to the long line.

1. Start with a 30-foot (9-m) cord or light rope attached to Buddy's collar. Pick a debris-free area to train and let the line drag on the ground.
2. Practice *heel*, *stay*, and *come*. If Buddy tries to run off, step on the long line to show that you have a long reach.
3. Practice daily for a few weeks with the long line. Then start cutting off a few inches of the line at a time, each week cutting off a foot or two of it. Buddy will not notice it getting shorter because you'll still be able to reach him.
4. Do not progress too rapidly with this. Soon enough, only a short handle of line will be attached to Buddy's collar, then nothing.

Commands in Daily Life

Use commands to direct Buddy's behavior in everyday situations.

■ When a pup jumps up, don't just push him away; teach him to *sit*.
■ When he begs at the table, don't banish him to the other room; teach him to hold a polite *down-stay* by your chair until your meal is over.
■ When you get ready to open the car door for a ride, command Buddy to *wait* before allowing him to hop in. He will learn to look to you as a leader.

Work on commands in different places and with varied distractions. Practice under different conditions so Buddy learns that commands always mean the same thing, no matter where they are given. Words are a foreign language to dogs. Be patient while Buddy learns commands and make sure he really understands what to do. Work as your dog's teacher, friend, and partner, not his adversary. Enjoyable lessons will be quickly learned.

Home Schooling

Sit

This may be the easiest command to teach and is a good start for a pup or new dog.

1. Show Buddy a small treat, raise it slightly above his head, and command *"Sit!"*
2. As Buddy's nose reaches higher, his rear should drop gently to a sitting position. Praise *"Good sit!"* and give him the treat.

The hand signal for *sit* starts at hip height with palm upward; then the open hand is raised in a smooth arc to about shoulder level. When using a lure, pinch it between your thumb and index finger and extend the rest of your fingers to show as much of your hand as possible. As Buddy follows the lure, he will automatically be learning the hand signal. Later, when you phase out the treat, you'll signal with a fully open, empty hand.

If Buddy does not sit for the lure, use gentle physical positioning to help him understand what you want.

1. Hold his collar or cup your hand under his jaw to raise his head slightly and prevent forward motion.
2. Stroke your other hand down his back, over his tail, and behind his rear legs.
3. When your hand is behind his stifles (knees), gently press forward, causing him to sit in your hand.
4. Lower his rear to the floor, slip your hand out from under him, praise *"Good sit!"* and pet him and offer the treat.

If a trained dog refuses a *sit* command, the gentle positioning method (above) can be used to correct him. Praise him when he sits, but do not give him a treat or he will expect food rewards for obedience and disobedience alike.

Down

1. Start with Buddy sitting.
2. Show him a treat, then very slowly lower it to the ground.
3. Let him lick and pick at the tidbit until he lies down. Some dogs will follow the food to the ground and lie down at

The pup will sit when he reaches for the treat above his nose.

The *down* command is easiest taught by using a treat lure; lower the treat to the ground.

once; others take a few tries to get it right. When first attempting the *down* with a lure, use no command; just lower the treat to the floor with the dog following it. When Buddy has successfully taken the *down* position three times, then you can give the command "*Down*" as you lower the lure.

If Buddy just bobs his head, following the treat lure, but does not lie down, determine the lowest point he will go and reward with the treat when he is there. Each time, lure him a bit closer to the ground before giving the treat. Encourage by praising him "*That's right*," or "*Good pup*," but do not say the praise phrase "*Good down*" until he has fully reached that position.

The hand signal for the *down* starts at the handler's head height with palm facing forward. Lower the hand to hip level in a smooth downward sweep. When training with a lure, exaggerate the hand signal at first so you end with your treat-holding signal hand on the floor just in front of Buddy's paws.

Puppy Pushups

A quick sequence of four or five *sit* and *down* commands, rewarded with treats, is fun for most energetic young dogs. When Buddy does "puppy pushups," he'll have fun practicing obedience.

Gentle Positioning

To use gentle physical positioning to teach the *down* or correct a refusal, start with Buddy sitting.

1. Kneel beside him and hold his collar.
2. Reach your other hand under the front leg nearest you and grasp the far leg just above his "wrist."
3. Lift both front legs, bent comfortably at the elbows, holding the far leg above the wrist and the near leg resting supported over your forearm.
4. Supporting the weight of Buddy's front end, lower his chest gently to the floor.

> **Note:** Consider your dog's strength and condition when asking for repetitions. Don't overdo pushups, especially with youngsters or senior dogs.

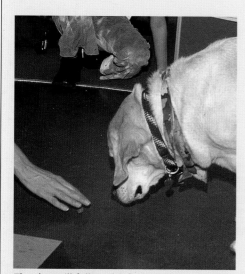

The dog will follow the food to the ground and lie down.

This method works great for cooperative dogs, but if yours is more rambunctious, try the following plan:

1. Kneeling at the right side of your sitting Lab, reach over his shoulders, hug him in to you, and grasp his far leg above the wrist. At the same moment, grasp his near leg above the wrist with your other hand.
2. Hugging the dog to you, lift both front legs—bent at the elbows—and slide Buddy down your knees to the floor.

A word on the *down* command from your dog's point of view: Lying down when commanded is a postural gesture signifying submission and low rank. Submissive dogs,

Note: *The height at which you hold the lure is important when teaching the stand command. If the treat is too high, Buddy will sit, and if it is too low, he'll lie down. It must be directly in front of the dog's nose, at the level it would be when standing, not above or below.*

when physically placed in the prone position, may display exaggerated submission by rolling over, averting their eyes, and even urinating. Dominant types often resent being physically placed into the *down* position and may fight, and even bite, the handler. For these reasons, the lure/reward method for teaching the *down* is almost always better than physical positioning.

Stand also can be taught with treat lures. Hold the treat in front of the dog's nose.

Praise the dog when he follows the lure.

Submissive dogs enjoy following treat lures, which makes the *down* position less threatening. Even dominant dogs will obey a *down* command to earn a treat. Unless Buddy has absolutely no interest in treats, use lures to teach this command. (*No* interest? Have you tried liver? Bacon? Hot dog or hamburger? Cat food? Breakfast Os? Cheesy puffs? Surely there's *something* Buddy can't resist. He *is* a Labrador!)

Stand

Stand is another position that can be taught with treat lures.

1. Start with Buddy sitting.
2. Show him a treat, then wiggle it and move it straight away from his nose.
3. When he stands to follow the lure, praise "*Good stand!*" and give the tidbit.

Be sure to give the reward while Buddy is actually standing. If he begins to sit before you can reward him, wiggle the lure and move it away so that he stands again. Praise and give the treat.

The hand signal for *stand* starts with your closed hand in front of Buddy's nose. Move your hand away at the same level, then stop, with your open palm facing the dog. This conveys the idea "*Move forward and stop,*" and as Buddy follows the lure/signal hand, he rises to a standing position.

If Buddy stands, then quickly sits again, he probably thinks you reward only dogs that sit. To solve this problem, lure him, with a treat, to a standing position while you slip your hand, open palm upward, below his

Give the treat.

Call your dog several times a day to give him a treat or toy; this will make "*Come*" a very positive word.

belly. Don't actually touch his tummy; just hold your hand an inch below it. Be very gentle—don't push or poke. Your hand should be a passive obstacle, so that if Buddy starts to sit, he will feel your hand and stand up. Praise and reward your good dog.

Come

Come may be the most important command, so start teaching it early. The younger Buddy is when you start him on *come*, the less resistance he will offer and the faster he will learn.

Most young puppies will run to you nearly every time they see you. Take advantage of this stage by associating the *come* command with this natural action. When little Buddy begins running toward you, give the command "*Buddy, come!*" Praise and pet him and give a treat. It's a lazy way to teach *come*, but it works. Each time you do this, Buddy's impulse to come when called will be strengthened.

Also call Buddy when he is mildly interested in something else. Do this when you don't really need him, just to reward him with petting, praise, and a treat or toy, then let him go back to what he was doing. Do this about ten times a day at odd intervals and soon Buddy will run to you whenever you call, expecting a treat, some good energy, and then going back to his earlier enjoyment.

You can start teaching the *come* command by calling your dog, then playfully starting to run away. When he follows, stop and give Buddy a treat, praising "*Good come!*" If he doesn't come when you first call, don't repeat yourself. Instead, start walking toward him. When he looks at you, move playfully away, enticing him to follow. Praise and reward with a treat when he comes close enough to be petted.

Outdoors, where there are numerous enticing distractions, you should teach *come* on leash first. After Buddy is proficient on leash, start practicing with a long line, preparing for off-leash work. Long-line training reminds a dog he <u>must</u> come when called, even when you are a distance away.

1. Attach a 30-foot-long (9-m) line to Buddy's collar and let him romp around while he gets used to the way it feels. Choose a training area free of brush or debris that could snag the long line.
2. While Buddy explores, give the *come* command.
3. If he responds, praise and reward him handsomely; if not, turn around and, holding the long line, run a distance

away. If he chases after you, allow him to catch up and praise him for coming. If not, when you reach the end of the line, Buddy will be turned around to face you, whether he means to or not. Give another *come* command, back away several steps to encourage him, and praise him when he obeys.

Stay

1. Start with Buddy sitting. Hold your open palm about a foot in front of his face for a moment and say "*Stay.*" Don't say his name when commanding "*Stay*" or Buddy might think you want him to come.
2. After signaling, take your hand away and stand erect. Wait one second, then praise "*Good stay!*" and give Buddy a treat. While he is eating the treat, give the hand signal and verbal *stay* command again, stand in front of him, wait three seconds, then praise and reward.
3. Repeat the exercise three or four times, adding a few seconds for each *stay* command, then release Buddy from the position, patting your leg and inviting him to move around. A dog should never release himself from a *stay*, but should always wait for permission, so don't forget to release him.

At this stage, do not call Buddy from a *stay* or his understanding of both "Stay" and "Come" may blur. Save the formal recall exercise (stay, come, finish) for later, when Buddy has learned the three parts separately. For now, simply invite him to get up and move.

For *stay*, teach both the hand signal and voice command.

After a few minutes, do another *sit-stay* session. Begin as before, but this time take one step away, then two, and have Buddy stay for five to ten seconds at the increased distance. Don't add more distance until Buddy can stay for ten seconds with you standing two steps away. After that, practice farther away and extend the time. Progress slowly. A little more time, a little more distance, and so on. If you go too fast, you'll confuse your dog. Gradually add distractions, building Buddy's skill and making practice sessions interesting challenges that he can successfully handle.

If Buddy moves while on a *stay*, immediately reposition him as he was when you left him. Praise him calmly for resuming his *stay* position, but do not reward with food or he may try breaking a *stay* just to get you to fix him and feed him. When he's doing solid *sit-stays*, teach *down-stay* and *stand-stay* too, using the same technique, rewarding gradual progress.

10 Tricks

Tricks and Obedience

Tricks are fun, and while Buddy learns to do tricks he will also be practicing obedience. Tricks are often more elaborate than simple obedience exercises but are surprisingly easy to teach, perhaps because both dog and handler enjoy themselves so much. Tricks can be so much fun that it is easy sometimes to get a bit carried away, so be careful not to ask Buddy to do anything that might injure him.

Treat lures are great to use for tricks, so don't hesitate to use them. Any position or action you can lure Buddy into with a treat can be put on command as a trick. You don't have to stick with ordinary commands for tricks. Use your imagination and make up amusing commands for tricks if you like. It won't matter one bit to Buddy what commands you use as long as you are consistent.

When teaching new tricks, don't introduce the command until you've lured your dog into position and rewarded him several times. After Buddy confidently follows the lure into a position, start using the command. When praising Buddy, use a short phrase that includes the command word, as in "*Good shake!*" This will speed his learning the new word.

Tricks can be useful or silly, but they should always be fun for the dog. Teaching Buddy tricks is a great way to engage his mind and his cooperation. Many tricks can also strengthen a dog's muscles, improve balance and coordination, and provide good exercise.

Treat lures and food rewards work well for teaching most tricks and make trick training sessions more fun for the dog. Trick training is also a great way for both dogs and handlers to learn the concept and techniques of clicker training.

If Buddy doesn't seem to enjoy a particular trick, work on one he likes better. Dogs, like the rest of us, enjoy showing off their favorite talents.

Clicker Training

The method known as clicker training involves a quick sound (usually a click) to *mark* the exact moment the dog does a desired behavior, which is then immediately followed by a treat reward. When the dog discovers that each click predicts a treat and that he can make clicks "happen" by doing particular behaviors, he'll happily learn to do those things.

Clicker training works with all types of animals, including all types of dogs. It encourages dogs to think and to cooperate. It's a completely nonforce method, so it's safe for even the youngest pup, and it doesn't rely on handler size or strength so can be used successfully by either adults or children.

This mark-and-reward style of training was used as early as the 1940s to train cats, crows, dolphins, and other animals to perform vital military-related tasks, from message carrying to espionage. The method made its main public debut with marine mammal trainers during the 1970s and was gradually picked up by dog trainers. By 2000, clicker training had gained many enthusiastic advocates because it's both effective and enjoyable, and it is now widely used to train not only companion pets but also many service dogs, police dogs, movie dogs, sport dogs, and show dogs.

A whistle is the most common behavior marker used with sea mammals, but in dog training it's the click of a small plastic noisemaker. Several styles of clickers are available through dog training schools and pet supply stores or web sites.

Though the method is called clicker training, a clicker device is not actually necessary. Suggested clicker alternatives are a short word (like "Yes!" or "Click!") or a tongue click or kiss sound. For hearing-impaired dogs you can use the flash of a flashlight (not a laser light, which can damage dogs' eyes) or a thumbs-up gesture. Any distinct sound or signal can be used as a marker—just choose one and stick with it. The timing of the marker is far more important than the type of marker used.

To accurately inform your dog that a behavior is "right," the marker must be

Clicker Training encourage dogs to think and to cooperate.

accurately timed to coincide with or immediately follow the behavior. For example, the absolute perfect timing for marking a *sit* would be *as if* the dog had sat on the clicker himself and made it click.

Your own observation and timing skills will determine how well mark-and-reward training works for you and your Lab. If your timing is good, your dog will quickly learn to do what you want him to do. If your timing is too far off, your dog will be confused. Fortunately, both observation and timing are skills that improve well with practice. Teaching tricks is a great way to learn and practice clicker training, because even if you're not very accurate at first, tricks are just for fun and are not vital skills. Teaching tricks will help you develop accurate observation and timing, and then you can use the techniques to teach your dog more complicated and important skills.

Home Schooling

Most people are simultaneously delighted and put at ease by watching a dog perform tricks. Here are a few tricks to get you started on the road to delighting an audience.

Shake

1. Start with Buddy sitting. Show him a treat. While he sniffs it, say *"Shake,"* or whatever command you've chosen for this trick, and pick up one of his front paws.
2. Touch the treat to the back of his paw for just a second, say *"Good shake,"* and feed him the treat.

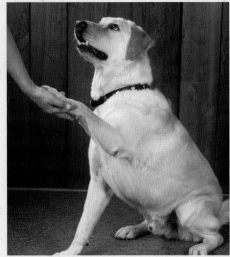
Teaching *shake* will make foot handling easier.

3. After you have lifted his paw and rewarded him about 10 or 20 times, say *"Shake,"* smile expectantly, and wait one second to see what Buddy will do. Some dogs immediately lift the paw without help; others take longer to get the idea.
4. Do the trick about ten more times, commanding, lifting the paw, and rewarding, then test again to see if just the command word and gesture will cue Buddy to raise his foot.
5. If he doesn't catch on after five or ten minutes, stop, and try again the next day. In a lesson or two, with encouragement and treats, Buddy will lift his paw when you say *"Shake."* When this happens, reward him heartily.

When Buddy can shake one paw, try going ambidextrous and teaching him to lift either paw on request. Say *"Shake"* and point to the paw you want. Be very obvious with your hand gesture, so Buddy clearly knows which foot you're indicating. Once he catches on, you'll be able to point at either front paw and he'll lift it.

Two cautions on *shake*: Pawing is a natural, doggie play gesture. Unexpect-ed, unsolicited pawing can scratch your arm or spill hot tea in your lap, so teach Buddy to shake only on command and refuse to touch the foot if Buddy offers this behavior on his own.

The other caution is that when you are shaking the paw, don't pump it up and down or wiggle it vigorously. As a courtesy to Buddy, just hold his paw warmly and move it gently. Dogs usually don't like power handshakes.

Sit Pretty/Beg

This trick is cute when performed by a big Lab.

1. Start with Buddy sitting squarely and let him sniff a treat.
2. Say *"Sit pretty"* or *"Beg,"* and raise the tidbit slowly until he barely lifts his front feet off the ground.
3. Click and feed him the treat. Praise *"Good sit pretty!"* or *"Good beg!"* as you're giving him the treat.
4. Repeat this several times, each time luring him a bit higher before you click and reward him.

Don't raise the treat too rapidly or Buddy will stand up or jump instead of balancing on his hindquarters. Also, while teaching this, don't lure him upright so fast that he tips over. If he starts to topple, be ready to ease his fall. At first, it may be helpful to stand behind him as you lure him upward. That way he can lean back against your legs for balance.

Once Buddy can balance on his own, teach him to hold the position longer before giving the treat. Three seconds is a fairly long time for a dog to remain in this position at first. *Sit pretty/Beg* demands balance and muscle strength, both of which take time to develop. Don't ask for too much too soon or Buddy may hurt his back.

Paws Up/Paws Down

1. Tap the edge of a chair with your fingers and tell Buddy *"Paws up."* Many dogs instantly respond by putting their paws where the fingers tapped. If he does, click, praise *"Good paws up!"* and give the treat. If he doesn't get it at first, encourage him excitedly to eat treats placed on the edge of the seat.
2. After rewarding Buddy for the *paws up* trick on the chair, show him another treat, then move it to the side, encouraging him to follow. Say *"Paws down,"*

The Sit Pretty trick teaches good balance.

lure him with the treat, click and reward him when he takes his feet off the chair.

3. Repeat the *paws up* and *paws down* sequence several times, luring and rewarding with treats, then try without the lure. Indicate with a hand motion (tapping) and give the command. If Buddy responds, reward with praise and treats. If he doesn't respond to the hand gesture alone, repeat, using a lure.

Jump Up/Jump Down

The technique for teaching this trick is similar to *paws up/paws down*, except you'll encourage Buddy to hop up onto something. A plank supported on cinder blocks would work well to start.

1. Show Buddy a treat and urge him to step or jump up onto the low platform. Say "*Jump up.*" Click and give him the treat when he puts one or both front feet on the plank.
2. Next, show Buddy another treat, which you should move downward and to the side as you command "*Jump down.*" Click an reward when Buddy follows the lure. Soon you'll be able to omit the lure and use only a hand signal or voice command. Once Buddy can perform the *jump up/jump down*, teach him to hop onto a sturdy chair and sit.

Say Prayers

Teach Buddy the *paws up* trick, then teach him to do it from a sitting position. This is more difficult than standing with paws up.

1. Sit him in front of a chair, tap the edge of the seat, and command "*Paws up.*" Encourage Buddy to keep his haunches on the ground by keeping your hand on his (sitting) rump as he raises his paws to the chair. Click, praise, and give a treat when he succeeds. Do this several times before introducing the new command: "*Say prayers.*"
2. Now, with Buddy in that position, lower the treat so his head is between his front paws. Click, praise, "*Good say prayers,*" and give the reward.
3. When Buddy will take the *say prayers* position on command, have him stay a few seconds before you click, reward, and give a release word. A fitting release command for *say prayers* might, of course, be "*Amen.*"

Catch

1. Show a soft ball or toy to Buddy, then wiggle it to make it really interesting.
2. Pantomime throwing the object before you toss, so Buddy will anticipate its arc.
3. Say "*Catch!*" and lightly toss the toy. If Buddy happens to catch it the first time, praise and celebrate with him a bit before taking the toy and throwing it again.

Some dogs quickly learn to catch, whereas others repeatedly let the toy hit them on the nose. Praise and encourage all catching attempts with lots of enthusiasm, even if Buddy misses. You can motivate some dogs to perfect their catch by tossing them popcorn one piece at a time. This is a fun way to learn, and doesn't hurt if it

Say Prayers is taught from a sitting position.

bounces off his nose instead of going into his mouth.

Treat on Nose/Flip Off and Catch

This trick teaches patience and steadiness.

1. The first part of the trick is teaching Buddy to balance the treat. A flat treat works best. Support Buddy's chin with one hand; your other hand gently holds a treat on the bridge of his nose.
2. Command "*Hold it.*" After a second, say "*Catch!*" and quickly hand him the treat.

After a number of repetitions you won't need to steady Buddy's head or hand him the treat; you can just brush it off his nose and he'll catch it. Perfor-

mance improves over time and some dogs become adept at flipping a treat up and snatching it from midair.

Jump

Most Labs enjoy leaping about, so it's not difficult to teach one to jump on command. "*Hup*" or "*Over*" are commonly used commands for this trick. Whatever command you use, say it with excitement to encourage your dog.

1. Start by holding a broomstick about 4 inches (10 cm) off the floor, across a doorway.
2. With a treat, lure Buddy to jump over the stick.
3. Click, praise, and give him the treat.
4. Toss another treat over and encourage Buddy to jump over and get it.
5. Gradually raise the stick as his strength and coordination grow.

Once Buddy knows the *jump* command, you can teach him to hop over a stick, your leg or arm, through a hoop, over your back, or over another dog—one with a trustworthy *down-stay*, we hope. Several types of competition—Agility, Rally, Rally flyball, advanced Obedience—require jumping, so if Buddy loves to leap, put it on command.

Jumping requires muscles and skills that take time to develop. Don't be in a rush to have Buddy jump too high or repetitively, as he could injure himself by landing wrong or straining too hard. Jumping is exciting and dogs keep going, not realizing they've injured themselves until the session is over. Labs are heavy as pups and sometimes a bit uncoordinated through adolescence. Most veterinarians recommend waiting until a dog is at least a year old before doing any serious jumping. Have your veterinarian examine Buddy thoroughly before you start him jumping.

Roll Over

1. Start with Buddy lying down. With a small treat, lure his head around toward his hip. When he turns as far as seems comfortable, click and give the treat.
2. Repeat, urging him to bend a little farther each time before giving the reward.
3. Eventually, he will start to tip slightly. Press the treat toward him farther as he nibbles at it.
4. At some point, gravity will take charge and he'll roll over onto his side, then

The Roll-Over trick teaches trust.

his back, then all the way over. Click, praise, and treat.

Some dogs are at first unwilling to roll over because the belly-up position is a vulnerable one. If Buddy is uncomfortable with this at first, keep working at it. Stay upbeat, give treats and praise, and soon Buddy will worry less about social connotations and just follow the treat lure.

Crawl

1. Start with Buddy in the *down* position. Kneel next to him and make a "bridge" with your arm over his head by placing the palm of your hand on the floor.
2. Give the command "*Crawl*" and, with your other hand, lure Buddy under the bridge with a treat. There will be no clearance for him to stand up, and Buddy will have to wiggle on his belly toward the treat.
3. Praise and reward.

When Buddy catches on to this trick, remove the arm bridge and just keep your hand above his shoulders as a "ceiling." Later, the command alone will cue Buddy to crawl and no bridge or ceiling will be necessary.

Speak

1. Teach "*Speak*" by showing Buddy a piece of popcorn, then saying "*Speak!*" in a crisp voice.
2. Next, "woof" in your most doglike tone, pause, then pop the treat into your

mouth. Chew, swallow, then hold up another piece of popcorn. Say *"Speak!"* and pause, then "woof" and eat.

3. Repeat this until Buddy vocalizes. It may be barely a breathy "huff" at first, but click and reward the slightest effort. Gradually hold out for louder barks before giving a treat.

Most dogs quickly get the idea of *"Speak!"* Some become overenthusiastic and try barking when they see you eating any snack, but you should reward *"Speak"* only when you command it, *never* when Buddy barks a demand.

Teach Buddy a silent signal to bark by pairing a hand gesture with the verbal command. The gesture should be distinct from normal movements. You could make the signal one that only Buddy will notice. A secret signal can add some fun to your life.

Whisper

Once you've taught *"Speak,"* teach Buddy to lower his voice to a quiet sound.

1. Do this by first commanding *"Speak!"* as you normally would. Reward his response.

2. Show a treat and say *"Whisper!"* Use a whisper when you command this and Buddy will soon mimic your quiet voice.

Buddy may bark loudly at first, before he understands this hushed variation of "Speak." If he barks loudly, pull the treat to your chest and turn your head to the side. Pause a moment, then again show Buddy the treat and whisper *"Whisper!"*

Sing

This is another variation on *"Speak,"* but instead of a bark you'll ask Buddy for a howl. This can usually be taught by simply howling yourself until Buddy gets excited and joins in. Dogs love a good group chorus, as their ancestors did, and most ask no other reward for the *"Sing"* trick beyond being allowed to do it.

Some dogs have a good ear for tones and will follow along, harmonizing with a simple note sequence. Some will sing when a harmonica or flute is played. Others start to howl when they hear a particular tune. Teach Buddy to sing along with "Happy Birthday"—great fun to leave on friends' answering machines.

Math Whiz

This is a trick to amaze your friends. With Math Whiz you'll ask Buddy to add or subtract figures and bark out the correct answer. Of course, you'll be cueing his barks with your secret hand signal.

To do this trick, ask Buddy, for example, "What's three plus two?" then cue him to bark five times. Be sure you know the right answer yourself, or Buddy—and you—will look foolish.

Tricks are fun and some can be useful. They help a dog burn energy and improve his response to commands. They can liven up an obedience session, amuse guests and friends, and delight children. Tricks add an enjoyable dimension to Buddy's training and will be fun for you both.

11 *Games and Family Fun*

Forming Life Skills Through Play

Dogs practice life skills through play, so how they play is important. This is especially true with puppies, as lessons learned while young will guide a dog for life. Tug-of-war, chase tag, and wrestling games that pit dogs against handlers create competition, not teamwork.

All training, including play-training, should remind your dog that you two are a team and you are the captain. Raise Buddy with games and toys fostering cooperation rather than competition, so habits he forms while playing will improve his relationship with you.

Good Toys/ Bad Toys

A good toy is durable, safe, and fun to play with. Dog toys should be easy to differentiate from non-toy items. Old shoes, socks, and gloves are not good toys, because they increase the likelihood that Buddy will chew your belongings. Dogs have no concept of price or value; they only know what feels good.

A pup in the teething stage—age four to eight months—needs to chew; therefore, provide a toy for each area or room in which your pup spends time. Encourage play with approved toys and make sure there is at least one appropriate chew toy available in every room. If Buddy makes a mistake and chews a forbidden item, calmly take it away from him, replace it with one of his permitted toys, and praise him for chewing that. If possible, put the wrongly chewed item out of Buddy's sight and reach for a day or two, so he's not tempted to immediately try to chew it again.

Here are some favorite dog toys:

- balls
- knotted ropes
- squeaky toys
- boat bumpers
- rubber or nylon chew bones

Several toys made of rubber or plastic have hollow centers into which food can be placed. The dog plays for hours, rolling, gnawing, and bouncing the toy as he tries to get the food out. Bits fall out intermittently, encouraging the dog's efforts. These toys keep the dog busy and exercise his jaws in an approved manner.

Some pups have so many toys they assume everything within reach is theirs.

Puppies need to chew on appropriate toys, especially during the teething stage.

If Buddy has an abundance of toys but still chews forbidden items, limit his toys for a month. Rotate the supply, keeping only three to five toys available at once.

Bones?

Bones are controversial chew toys. For centuries all dogs were given bones from the master's table; chewing bones was considered part and parcel of being a dog. The only bones owners usually denied their dogs were poultry leg and wing bones that could splinter and perforate an unfortunate dog's intestines. Starting around 1970 veterinarians, breeders, and other experts began switching their dogs from bones to nylon or rubber chew toys that were considered much safer for a dog's teeth and digestion. Bones were considered hazardous.

More recently, opinions on bones have changed again. Though some experts still warn against giving any bones at all, others point out that raw bones and meat are an important part of a healthy natural diet for dogs. Meanwhile, others say that bones must be slow-cooked to remove excess fat and prevent bacterial growth. Confused? No wonder! If you are undecided, ask your veterinarian for guidance on bones. In any case, be sure Buddy does not swallow large or sharp bone chunks, as these have been known to cause digestive upset or internal blockage.

Games for the Whole Family

The dog is a great equalizer of human beings. Rich or poor, old or young, dog lovers become playful when invited by a wiggly pup or grinning dog. That playfulness is one of the great benefits of dog ownership.

Games are fun and also teach important lessons. Good games teach positive social skills, but some games can teach bad manners. Make sure you do not inadvertently teach Buddy the wrong things in play. Teach games that are not only fun and active, but that help Buddy learn gentleness, cooperation, and control.

The activities that follow can be exciting for a dog, but care should be taken that the children and the dogs follow the rules so that the games teach positive behaviors. Make sure that dogs and children do not get carried away while playing and accidentally hurt each other. For safety's sake, young children and dogs should never be left to play together without adult supervision.

Thank You/Take It

This game teaches your dog to take an object gently and then release it when asked. The commands for this game were selected for their polite sound. If you prefer to use different commands (such as "*Give*" or "*Drop*") the game will still work. Choose a toy large enough for your Lab to hold one end while you hold the other. A plush toy or knotted rope would work well.

1. Liven up the toy by shaking it and wiggling it around to entice Buddy to go after it. When he shows interest, say "*Take it,*" and let him grab on. Continue holding the toy and moving with him as he mouths and plays with it for five to ten seconds.

> **Note:** *A caution is necessary about tug. Even tug-of-peace can cause problems if played too vigorously. Although the frequent pauses with release of the toy prevent Buddy from learning bad habits, rough tugging can cause physical problems. Teeth can misalign if too much force is used in tug, especially with pups and young adults. Also, too-vigorous pulling or shaking of the toy by the human player can cause neck strain in young or out-of-condition dogs. Tug-of-peace is a valuable game, but should be played with moderation.*

2. Then stop moving your hand around and hold still. Say "*Thank you,*" and show your Lab a treat in your other hand about 6 inches (15 cm) away from the side of his mouth. Most dogs will opt for the treat and let go of the toy.
3. When Buddy lets go, praise "*Good thank you*" and give him the treat as a reward. Don't move the toy away when Buddy lets go.
4. As soon as he finishes the treat, offer the toy back, saying "*Take it!*" Praise "*Good take it!*" He'll realize he doesn't lose his toy when he gives it up to you.

Repeat this several times, ending with "*Take it*" and allowing Buddy to keep the toy. Everyone wins in this game!

Tug-of-Peace

Most professional trainers agree that tug-of-war is a bad game that teaches a dog to compete against his handler. Many advise not to play tug at all because the game can become too aggressive. Although that's true of the old no-holds-barred tug-of-war, tug-of-peace is different and sends nearly the opposite message. Tug-of-war teaches the dog to compete against the handler, which is never good; tug-of-peace teaches Buddy to cooperate and control himself, even when highly excited—this is always good.

This game is very stimulating, so go easy at first, allowing the rules of the game to sink in.

1. Begin tug-of-peace by playing Thank You/Take It, then escalate the excitement by encouraging Buddy to tug on the toy a bit before you ask for it back.

A game of fetch is good exercise and prepares a dog for performance events.

(Remember: The command to release is "*Thank you.*")

2. When Buddy releases, praise, then command him to take the toy and begin the game again.
3. Each round of the game can have a different tug-force level. Teach Buddy to pull only as hard as you want him to by letting the toy slip through your fingers when he pulls too hard. If you let go that way, without trying to fight his strength, Buddy will not feel he has "won" a competition, but that he's lost the playmate at the other end of the toy. Most dogs that have learned Thank You/Take It will quickly give the toy back when it slips from your hand.

Fetch

A game of fetch can provide good exercise for your dog without exhausting you. Most Labs will chase a ball or stick as often as it's thrown and, with a little training, deliver the object to hand. Labs as young as five weeks may show natural retrieving ability.

1. To begin teaching fetch, show Buddy a toy, wiggle it, then toss it a few feet away. Encourage him to get it and praise if he picks up the toy, but don't ask him to bring it back yet. Just let him enjoy the toy.
2. If he carries the toy to you, don't reach for the object. If you do, you'll give the object too much value and Buddy may not want to give it up.

3. Pet the dog, then say "*Thank you*" and take the toy.
4. Praise, then shake the toy and toss it again. Encourage your dog to get it.
5. When Buddy picks up the object, clap your hands and walk away playfully. If your dog follows, carrying the toy, stop moving. If he brings the toy, praise.

When Buddy consistently brings the toy to you, teach him to return the object directly to hand:

1. Throw as usual, but when Buddy brings it, offer your open palm as a delivery target. Do not reach for the object; just wait patiently with your hand open. Don't stare at Buddy or the fetch item;

just look at your open hand. This will draw your dog's attention to your hand, where you want him to put the item.

2. If your dog drops the toy, playfully encourage him to pick it up and put it in your hand. Accept only retrieves that at least touch your hand.

3. If your dog teases and tries to get you to chase, don't fall for that old trick. Buddy wants to play this game more than you do and will ultimately play by your rules.

If you get bored waiting for Buddy to deliver the toy, sit and read a magazine while you play. Throw the toy, then lay your hand in your lap, palm up and open, ready to receive. Ignore Buddy until you feel the object in your hand, then smile, praise, and toss the toy again. With the hand-delivery rule in effect, Buddy will realize that if he wants to play, he has to give you the toy.

Some Labs become fixated on one particular toy. To prevent this, vary the fetch toy so the object itself does not become an obsession. To make the game challenging for Buddy and more interesting, teach names for his toys, such as big ball, squeaky frog, and so on, and then ask for a specific one. Once Buddy is past the teething stage you could teach him to fetch your slippers or newspaper. Most Labs can also learn to pick up dropped items and retrieve them to hand.

Go Find

This is fun for all ages of dogs and people. It can also be useful.

1. Begin by having someone hold Buddy while you hide nearby. Wait a minute, then call him.

2. Pet and give a food reward when he finds you. Make it easy at first; early success is encouraging.

3. Now hold Buddy while your assistant hides. Wait a minute, then tell him "*Go find Susie* (or whomever)" and release him to search for her. Have Susie give Buddy a treat when he finds her, and you do the same. Then it's your turn to hide again.

Go Find can also be played with a hidden object:

1. At first, hide it while Buddy watches. Send him to find the item by name ("*Go find Fuzzy Bear*").

2. Start by using Buddy's toys; later have him find other small objects, such as a ring of keys or a wallet.

Go Wild and Freeze

This game is fun and useful for a family with young children and a boisterous dog. Go Wild and Freeze teaches an "off switch" for rowdy behavior in both species of youngsters. An adult human should control this game until all players know and respect the rules.

Start by teaching Buddy to sit using a treat lure, then teach the children how to command their pet to sit for reward. Once this groundwork is laid, the game may begin.

1. On your signal—"*Go wild!*"—everyone hops and waves and runs around making happy noises.

2. After a few seconds, call *"Freeze!"* All players stop and stand up tall. Whomever Buddy is closest to commands him to sit, then gives a treat. Timid children may need extra help controlling the dog.
3. After the reward is given, the game begins again with *"Go wild!"*

Each round can last a bit longer before stopping the action. Five seconds is long enough for the first few; more than that and players may become too excited to follow rules. Call "Freeze" before that happens.

This game will teach Buddy to sit instead of jumping and to stop when commanded. It also teaches children to control the dog when he's excited.

First teach your pup to sit, then play Go Wild and Freeze.

Go Play/Come Away

This is a cooperation game that will strengthen Buddy's habit of coming when you call him, even when he's playing with doggie pals or people friends. You'll need plenty of yummy treats for this game. An assortment that includes several of Buddy's favorites would be best.

Tell Buddy to *"Go play."* Let him enjoy a nice sniff in the grass or a few minutes playing with a dog or human friend. Go to Buddy and show him a yummy treat. Put it right in front of his nose, then wiggle the treat back and forth while moving it away from him, like a fish swimming away. Tell Buddy *"Come away,"* enticing him to follow the treat. Use the cookie-right-on-the-nose technique only until your Lab figures out how the game works and starts moving toward you on his own when he hears *"Come away."* After that,

stop using the treat as a lure—don't show it to him when you call, just reward him with it when he gets to you.

When Buddy starts to move toward you, praise him *"Good come away!"* and give him the treat while holding his collar gently with your other hand. Tell Buddy *"Go play,"* and release him to go back to his pals or other fun.

Play this game when Buddy is romping with other dogs, socializing with human friends, or sniffing the trail ahead of you on walks. ALWAYS reward for *"come away"* so your Lab will enjoy forming this positive habit. This will teach him to come quickly and willingly whenever you call, regardless of what else he's doing. He will realize he doesn't lose anything by coming to you. In fact, he gets a double reward—he gets a tasty treat and also gets to go back to his fun.

Hiking and camping are fun activities to share with your Labrador.

Fun Outdoor Activities with the Family

Camping

Camping is a dog's idea of the ideal vacation because his people go outside and live in nature, the way he'd like them to live. There's a broad range of camping styles to choose from: cabins, RVs, tents, and developed or primitive campsites. Any campout is fun for a dog, and with appropriate training, Buddy can learn to enjoy himself without spoiling the outing for the rest of the family.

Before you go camping, train Buddy to walk politely on leash. Although you'll be in the great outdoors, Buddy must be under control to avoid trouble and danger. He should also learn to accept being tethered, as he may have to be confined that way in camp unless you can take along a folding pen.

Before heading out, call ahead to make certain dogs are welcome at the campsite. Many campgrounds allow well-behaved, leashed pets, but not all do. Check regulations for state and national parks and forest reserves—some allow leashed dogs; others forbid pets entirely. Check during the earliest planning stages; don't wait to find out when you're already there.

Day Hikes and Picnics

Take along enough food for both you and Buddy, plus warm clothes, first aid supplies, and a reflective emergency blanket in case you must stay out longer than intended. Water is important when hiking, and you should carry enough for Buddy too. Lakes and streams that harbor nasty microorganisms can make dogs ill, as well as humans, so don't allow Buddy to drink from a questionable water source.

Note: Do not let Buddy run loose in camp. For one thing, it's probably against the law, but more important, it can be dangerous. Loose dogs bother other campers, chase wildlife and livestock, roll in excrement, get sprayed by skunks or quilled by porcupines, become lost, fall off cliffs, drown, and meet other horrible fates. Don't put Buddy at risk by turning him loose.

Teach your big, strong Lab to wear a doggie backpack. Dogs love their packs when properly introduced to them. Start training Buddy with the pack empty, adding weight a bit at a time over a week or so, until he can comfortably carry the load he will bear on the trail. Buddy could probably carry his own food and water and possibly some of yours. Don't overload him, though, or his back may be injured.

Be sure the pack fits properly. If it is too loose or too tight, Buddy will be miserable with his pack rubbing, chafing, and sliding around. Also, be sure to load his pack with equal weight in both panniers so it balances properly. Too much weight on one side will cause the pack to slip, which is uncomfortable and may throw the dog off balance.

Unless he is extremely well trained, keep Buddy leashed while hiking or picnicking; it's too risky to let him run free and may also break the law.

Boating Fun and Safety

Labs are fabulous water dogs and can enjoy boating as much as their owners do. Even though Labs are strong swimmers, have Buddy wear a flotation vest while boating in rough water or far from shore. Accidents can happen and some extra buoyancy can save a dog's life. Water safety vests for dogs of all sizes are available from pet supply stores and catalogs.

Teach Buddy to hold a reliable *sit-stay* and *down-stay*. These are very important commands both ashore and afloat. A dog that will not obey a *stay* command could cause a canoe or dingy to capsize.

Labs can learn good boating manners.

The Lab's ancestral duties included retrieving fish and hauling nets ashore. If Buddy will retrieve sticks or bumpers from the water, he could also learn useful skills such as rescuing swimmers or towing small boats to shore.

1. Once Buddy will fetch floating objects to you while you stand on shore, teach him to bring things to you while you are in the water, then stand in the water waist deep and have your helper on the beach give Buddy a boat bumper with a few feet of rope attached.
2. Call Buddy out into the water, encouraging him to bring the bumper. Praise happily when he reaches you, then, holding the rope while Buddy holds the bumper, swim back to shore with him. Have your helper call and encourage the dog toward shore.
3. When you get there, both you and your helper should praise and make a happy fuss over Buddy.

As he catches on, make the game gradually more challenging. Swim out into deeper water, then have your helper send Buddy to you with the bumper. When this becomes easy, stand on shore and have your helper swim out, then send Buddy to "rescue" your helper with the bumper and line.

Later, lengthen the rope line and exchange the bumper for a life ring. Teach Buddy to hold the rope and tow the ring. When he can do that, teach him to pull a small boat by a line to the bow. Buddy will get good exercise with these maneuvers and learn skills that—who knows?—might make him a hero one day.

Parades, Walkathons, Community Fun

Dog walkathons to raise money for charities have become popular in many areas.

Owners sign up to walk or run several miles with their dogs and get friends and coworkers to sponsor their efforts, with proceeds going to worthy causes. Leash-trained dogs with friendly attitudes can have fun on these charity walks. Bring plastic bags for picking up dog waste—they're bound to be needed on a long walk with a bunch of dogs. Also bring water to drink along the way.

Holiday parades, especially in small towns, often welcome groups of all sorts to march. You and a few dog-walking friends could probably come up with a group name and some sort of amusing costume or uniform and walk together in the next parade. Again, be sure to carry drinking water and pickup bags.

Many communities hold seasonal outdoor celebrations. Dogs are often welcome to attend these—on leash of course—if they have good manners and are not nervous in crowds. Aggressive dogs don't belong at large gatherings, nor do very timid dogs, so consider Buddy's temperament when deciding whether to take him to the fair.

There are many games and activities you and your family can enjoy with your well-behaved Lab. The more things Buddy learns to do, the more fun you can have with him. Training Buddy in obedience and social skills will give him the good start he needs to become a wonderful companion. Sharing life's fun with him will bring you years of pleasure.

The more your Lab learns, the more fun you'll have together.

12 Building Your Lab's Confidence

A well-bred, well-raised Lab will go through life without undue worry, knowing that the world, though full of surprises, is not a hostile place. New or unusual situations will produce curiosity, but not anxiety, in a dog with good early socialization and training.

Sensitive Periods

There are emotionally sensitive periods that every dog goes through during puppyhood. At those times Buddy may seem low in confidence and easily worried. One of these stages occurs at around six weeks, another at three months, another at five months. During these periods a daring pup may become less outgoing and more shy, as well as more easily frightened.

Puppyhood should be a fairly protected time, as dogs' minds are as fragile as their bodies in the first half year. During sensitive phases avoid exposing Buddy to stressful new situations; instead, work on activities he already does well, to help build his confidence.

Fear of the Unknown

Most Labs are intrigued by novelty, but some fear it. In most cases anxiety is based on insufficient exposure to new situations. Avoiding new situations prevents positive experiences as well as negative ones. If a dog shies away from all novelty, he feeds his fear-driven belief that avoidance keeps him safe.

Fears seldom disappear on their own, but can often be cured by presenting positive experiences that prove to Buddy that the feared situation is harmless. Do make certain something really is harmless before trying to reassure Buddy that it is. If a feared situation actually proves injurious, Buddy's confidence and trust in you will drop.

Promoting Trust

One of your jobs as Fearless Leader is teaching Buddy to trust you and obey you under varied circumstances. This is necessary for safety and also to better enjoy his company. Trust training can be accomplished in a mutually enjoyable way with some simple tricks.

Belly Up (Lie on Back)

The belly-up position infers submission in a doggie hierarchy. Rolling over is normally offered to appease a higher-ranking dog. Most Labs can be cajoled into rolling upside down for a tummy rub, but some are hesitant or unwilling to take such a vulnerable position. Buddy needs to learn to trust that you won't ever do anything to hurt him and that he's safe in your hands, even in a vulnerable belly-up position.

Teach Buddy to lie on his back by teaching him to roll over (see page 76). This will have both psychological and physical benefits: It teaches a fun trick, demonstrates Buddy's trust, and allows you access to examine or groom his underside. This training reduces the symbolic value of an exposed underbelly, which helps submissive dogs worry less and dominant dogs comply better.

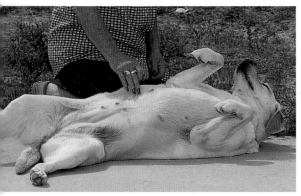

Relaxing belly up builds trust.

Mouth Handling

A well-trained companion dog must allow examination of his mouth, yet never lay his teeth on human skin. The Labrador Retriever is generally a gentle-mouthed breed, but poor early social-ization can lead to nipping and biting.

To avoid mouth-on-flesh encounters, teach your puppy gentle mouth manners from his earliest days. Never allow Buddy to play mouth-on-hand games or chew on you—not even once. Nippy puppy games can mature into aggressive antisocial behavior.

Every time little Buddy starts to mouth your hands, immediately say *"Ow!"* in a very serious tone. Do not pull away; just freeze and glare at the pup for a moment, then pause, relax, gently pet Buddy, and calmly praise him. If he mouths you again, repeat the *"Ow!"* treatment, then either walk away and ignore him or put him in his crate for a five-minute time-out.

Don't let other people teach Buddy aggressive play habits, either. If friends or family members roughhouse with Buddy, stop them immediately. An uninformed game can ruin weeks of good training.

Calming Massage

Some Labs are so exuberant and wiggly when receiving attention that they are difficult to pet and nearly impossible to examine. Teach Buddy to hold still for cuddling, grooming, and health care by massaging him (see page 46).

When you first start massaging your dog he may wiggle and try to escape.

Hang on and do not allow him to squirm loose. This teaches Buddy to be relaxed under your hand and to allow touch anywhere. Some dogs have other ideas at first, but with a daily ten- to fifteen-minute massage, any dog can learn to hold still.

Easy Agility Obstacles

Agility obstacles are fun and build confidence for pups and mature dogs alike. The sport of Agility has grown tremendously because dogs and handlers enjoy it so much. As Buddy learns to negotiate the jumps, planks, tunnels, platforms, and seesaws of Agility, his confidence and physical coordination will improve. You can easily make a few "baby" Agility obstacles to give you and Buddy a taste of the fun and teamwork of this growing sport.

Build agility and confidence by walking along a slightly elevated plank.

- Make an elevated walkway for Buddy by supporting both ends of a plank 6 to 12 feet (1.8–3.6 m) long, 12 inches (30 cm) wide, and 2 inches (5 cm) thick on bricks or blocks. Start just a few inches off the ground so Buddy will not be injured or frightened if he accidentally steps off. Lure him onto one end of the plank by holding a treat a few inches above the center line and moving it forward until all four of Buddy's feet are on the board, then lure him to walk along by holding a treat right in front of his nose, over the midline of the plank. Before Buddy steps off the far end of the plank, say "Wait," stop him, and give him a treat, then tell him to step down. Praise for stepping down, but don't give a treat, as that may make him too eager to jump off. When Buddy can walk along that plank without stepping off until he reaches the end, add a second plank. Lay the planks end to end, resting one end of each plank on a cinder block laid on its side, so the planks form a low bridge. Have Buddy walk up one plank and down the other, which will get him used to working on inclined ramps. When he's comfortable doing this, add some height to increase steepness by stacking a second cinder block atop the first one.

- Create a seesaw obstacle by balancing the midpoint of a plank crossways on a 6-inch (15-cm) diameter log or pipe. Seesaws are scary for some dogs, especially as they pass over the balance point and the plank suddenly begins to tilt down. When starting Buddy on this obstacle, steady the plank as he passes over the balance point, then ease the end down instead of letting it drop.

- A low jump can be made by resting the ends of a broomstick on blocks 4 inches (10 cm) high. Place this jump across a doorway at first and coax Buddy to follow as you step over, then toss a treat over and send Buddy after it. Practice having Buddy stay beside you until you give him a command to jump over the bar. Try sending him to fetch a toy over the jump.

Keep the jumps low and obstacles easy for Buddy as he grows. Once his body matures, at about a year, you could start him on regulation Agility obstacles. For more on Agility trials, see page 120.

Working Through Fears

Most fears are caused by lack of exposure or by unpleasant previous experience. To desensitize a dog's reactivity, expose him to the feared object or situation in a closely controlled way. Be careful not to scare a worried dog worse by carelessness during desensitization. Build Buddy's confidence in your ability to keep him safe in a situation that makes him nervous. A dog with faith in his handler is less prone to anxiety.

Fear of Sounds

- Thunder is one noise that sends many dogs running to hide. Thunder fear is usually worse when the dog's owner is also afraid of storms; owner fear reac-

tions cue dogs to be more afraid. Nature recordings are available that have storm sounds interwoven with soothing music. These can be used to accustom a dog to thunder in a non-threatening way. Teach Buddy that thunder is harmless by playing a recording of it quietly in the background while he naps or enjoys a chew bone. Gradually increase the volume to a realistic level. Be sensitive to Buddy's reactions; remember, a dog's hearing is many times keener than ours. Allow Buddy to become relaxed at each heightened volume before making it louder again. Slow progress is best. If you increase the volume too quickly, Buddy may become more fearful, not less.

- Fear of vacuum cleaners seems like a silly phobia but it's very real for many dogs. Perhaps it is the machine's high whine or the sound of small objects clattering up the tube, but vacuum cleaners can apparently seem like scary monsters to a dog. Reduce this fear by leaving the machine out where the dog can see and smell it while it's safely silent. Drop a few treats around the machine to tempt Buddy closer and encourage exploration. When the machine's silent presence no longer worries the dog, turn the cleaner on and off a few times. Then, when the sound no longer startles Buddy, turn it on and let it run. Don't vacuum the floor; simply sit down and read a magazine. This demonstrates that you consider the noise normal and nonthreatening. Toss a few treats on the floor near your feet and wait for

Buddy to eat them. Then toss some a bit closer to the vacuum cleaner and ignore Buddy. When he eats those, toss a few more. After Buddy eats those, turn off the vacuum cleaner and read for a few more minutes before ending the "session."

■ To prevent fear of gunfire in a potential hunting dog, accustom him to the sound at a distance first. Take him to a safe spot a half mile or so from an outdoor target range and play on leash there. Give treats, toss a ball, whatever the dog usually enjoys. The distant background sound of gunfire will become linked in your dog's memory with an enjoyable outing. Don't overdo exposure; close gunfire can cause permanent hearing loss in dogs and humans.

Fear of Fireworks

The sound of fireworks, especially the types that whistle loudly or finish with a ground-shaking boom, upsets many dogs. Some dogs even fear the sight of fireworks blossoming in the night sky. In most areas fireworks displays happen only a few times a year, so dogs seldom have a chance to get used to them on their own. New Year's Eve fireworks displays are televised in many areas, though, so if you can record that from your television and play it back occasionally, you may be able to help Buddy become accustomed to those startling sounds and sights. Cook up a bowl of popcorn to share with Buddy and sit down with him to watch the recording.

Start with the sound turned off, so there's only the visual effect, and play a musical recording in the background. Toss a handful of popcorn on the floor for Buddy to graze on. Don't turn up the sound of the fireworks until the sight of them doesn't upset Buddy. Then start playing the soundtrack of the fireworks so quietly that you can hardly hear it. Continue to play the musical recording as well. Occasionally scatter more popcorn for Buddy. If he eagerly cleans up the popcorn and looks to you for more, that means he's beginning to relax about the fireworks.

As Buddy relaxes and accepts seeing and hearing the recorded fireworks, gradually turn up the sound until it's at a realistic level and keep tossing popcorn. Play the recorded fireworks for about a half hour, and then turn them off.

Treat Buddy to a weekly "night at the movies" with popcorn and a half hour of recorded fireworks. After a few exposures to it, Buddy will probably relax and may even begin ignoring their sounds and sight. Keep the recording handy, and when you know there will be real fireworks, hold a "fireworks movie night" complete with popcorn for Buddy.

Most dogs can lose their fear of fireworks, but if you're not able to help Buddy stop panicking when he hears them, ask your veterinarian if it would be a good idea to medicate him on the nights when there are common fireworks displays. Many dogs who fear fireworks will panic and run away, trying to escape them, and some of those dogs get hit by cars or become disoriented and lost. If you must leave Buddy home alone during fireworks displays, be sure he's securely confined.

Teach your pup that the vacuum cleaner is not to be feared.

the hair is shorter. A dog with sensitive skin may fear having his face or other tender places brushed. Try a softer brush, chamois cloth, or grooming mitt. When grooming feels good, a dog can learn to like it.

Fear of Paw Handling

Toenail cutting is another matter; few dogs look forward to this procedure. In a dog's nails there are blood vessels and nerves that are sensitive to pain and can be accidentally injured by being trimmed too close. If a dog worries when his feet are handled, it becomes more difficult to trim his nails safely. Teach Buddy to allow gentle paw handling so he will not fear nail care.

Begin by "holding hands" and gently fussing with Buddy's paws during a relaxing massage. Teaching "*Shake*"(page 72) will also speed acceptance of foot handling. This is easiest if you start when he's young, but it can also be done with a grown dog. If Buddy learns to associate comfortable massage with foot handling, he will be less anxious.

To clip Buddy's nails, utilize his relaxation during massage. Trim just one nail each day at first if he's very anxious about it. Some dogs initially react fearfully, but with patience, you can teach any dog to accept gentle foot care. Don't worry about trimming each nail to a perfect length while doing the desensitization training; it's better to trim too little than too much.

Fear of Objects

To reduce Buddy's suspicion about an unfamiliar object, touch the object yourself, then let him smell your hand. This shows you are not afraid of the object and allows him a whiff of its scent. If he wants to sniff the object directly, encourage and approve—if it's safe. Keep the encouragement low key or Buddy, sensing exaggerated cheerfulness, may become more suspicious. Make certain when encouraging exploration of the feared object that Buddy is not hurt by it.

Fear of Grooming

A Lab's coat is short and never tangles, so most enjoy a good brushing. The exception may be on the legs and face, where

Fear of People

Most Labs consider strangers to be friends they haven't met yet, but some Labs can develop a fear of certain types of people. These fears often stem from unfortunate encounters during puppyhood. The original scary person may be long gone, but the dog may continue to fear all people resembling the original "scary" one. Delivery people, skateboarders, people in uniform, and children under ten are groups that seem to rate high on the doggie fear scale.

To prevent or reduce fear of people, take Buddy on leash to places where he can observe people from a nonthreatening distance. Move gradually closer as his anxiety decreases, until he can tolerate being quite close. Let him make friends with some of the people, if possible. Do not pressure him to go closer than he feels comfortable, and don't let people rush up to him; a dog that perceives himself cornered may bite in self-defense.

If Buddy is shy when a visitor comes to your home, help put him at ease by shaking hands with or hugging your visitor. This demonstrates that you like and trust the person. Let Buddy sniff your hands to get the scent of the welcome visitor. The scent superimposed on your own will probably put your dog at ease.

Hand your guest some treats that Buddy particularly enjoys and ask the person to toss or drop them on the floor for Buddy one at a time. If Buddy warms up to the visitor and approaches in a friendly manner, the person can hand-feed him some treats. Caution your guest not to reach to pat fearful Buddy until the dog sniffs or licks the visitor's hands and

behaves in a relaxed way that makes it obvious he would enjoy the contact.

Most shy dogs normally prefer to be ignored by visitors until the owner and guests have greeted. This allows the dog to observe from a safe distance until he determines that the new person is not a threat. After that, a shy dog may be willing to greet a visitor.

Fear of Other Dogs

Puppyhood is the best time for a dog to learn to get along with other dogs. Early canine playmates can result in a life filled with play pals. Pups separated too early from mother and siblings, before learning basic dog manners, may not read dog language as clearly as those with more experience. These pups may have trouble forming skills for getting along with their own kind, and have difficulty making friends with their fellow dogs. Puppy kindergarten classes can help a great deal with this as can play sessions at a well-run doggie day care. Be sure to let Buddy meet and play with other gentle, healthy dogs as he grows.

A mature Lab that fears other dogs may snap at any that come close, making him difficult to socialize. He will need to learn new behavior or fear and fighting may ruin your outings. Private sessions to teach commands and build confidence are recommended to start with, then add group sessions with selected dogs for experience in canine company. Once Buddy becomes more optimistic when meeting dogs, you can gradually increase his social exposure. Ask your veterinarian to refer you to a trainer or behaviorist

Let your Lab meet and play with other dogs.

who is experienced in working with anxious dogs.

Come away is a good training exercise for practicing socialization skills (see page 28). Make a habit of interrupting Buddy's play with pleasant treats and praise, then letting him return to his fun. Buddy will become more obedient to your call and gain social confidence as well.

Fear of Vehicles

Cars and trucks are big, noisy, fast, and smelly, all qualities that make them scary to some dogs. Reality-based caution

around vehicles is important and can prevent injuries, but excessive fear can cause harm. A terrified dog escaping from one car might dash under the wheels of another. Teaching proper behavior around vehicles will preserve Buddy's safety, reduce his anxiety, and make travel more pleasant for you both.

If Buddy is afraid of vehicles, note which situations make it worse. Begin antianxiety training in low-fear situations and work up gradually to scarier ones.

If Buddy's fear is primarily of the sound of cars, make an audiotape of traffic noise and play it quietly while Buddy naps or quietly chews a bone. As his anxiety decreases, increase the volume until Buddy ignores the sound.

If the sight of approaching vehicles triggers Buddy's fear, find a safe place near the side of the road where you and he can stand and watch cars together. On rural roads have the dog practice *sit-stay* as cars go by. In city environments just stand or sit with your dog in a safe spot near traffic for 10 or 15 minutes every day for a week and feed him tasty treats as cars go by. If he is too worried to eat the treats you give him, move a bit farther away and try again. Gradually move closer as Buddy's anxiety lessens. Fears will be replaced by confidence as Buddy learns that the cars are not really chasing him.

To relieve or prevent unreasonable fears, teach your dog that he can always trust you to keep him safe. As Buddy's confidence in your leadership grows, his own self-confidence will also increase.

13 Overcoming Behavior Problems

Handling Bad Habits

A puppy starts life with a clean slate and no bad habits. Although basic temperament and certain behaviors have an inherited potential, each new activity a pup attempts must be learned and practiced. If you keep a close watch as Buddy tests new behaviors, you'll be able to encourage positive activities and discourage disallowed ones before they become bad habits.

Problem habits are largely preventable through proper early socialization and training. A dog can develop a pattern of misbehavior, however, that may seem harmless and remain unnoticed until it reaches problem proportions. Then a remedy must be found.

Simply punishing a naughty act will not usually eliminate it. To defeat a bad habit it is important to prevent its occurrence while simultaneously teaching better behavior through consistent training and practice. It's harder to change a bad habit than to form a good one, although the training concept is similar.

Management is a powerful tool to prevent your Lab from forming bad habits, especially during puppyhood, when he's learning new skills at warp speed. If you

manage Buddy's comings and goings and keep him with you or safely confined, he won't get into the habit of wandering off. If you control the kinds of situations that might tempt him to misbehave, it will be much easier to help him develop good, trustworthy house manners. Keep shoes put away when you're not wearing them so your pup won't discover he likes their flavor. Don't leave your sandwich or cookie on the coffee table when you go to the kitchen for a glass of milk. If he gets into the bathroom trash once, make sure he doesn't do it a second time. Don't just make it a bit more difficult for him to reach—make it impossible. The more times Buddy succumbs to a particular temptation the more likely he is to do the same thing again. Repetition is how habits—both good and bad—are formed.

To form a good habit, Buddy must be shown what to do and his cooperation must be repeatedly rewarded. Good training makes a new behavior seem desirable to the dog, but some enjoy their old bad habits so much that it's hard to give them up. When praise and rewards for the new behavior are not quite enough motivation for Buddy, appropriate punishment can be used to make the naughty behavior less appealing.

Correction and Punishment

Many people assume that correction and punishment are the same; they are different, although their edges sometimes blur. *Correction* helps a dog perform the right behavior, as with physically placing him in position. *Punishment* dramatizes the consequences of a wrong act, as with a scolding or time-out. Without corrections, to show the dog the right path, punishments will yield no benefit and may, in fact, make him fear his handler and the lesson.

Proper socialization and training early in life will help prevent bad habits.

Punishment makes absolutely no sense if Buddy doesn't fully understand what you want and exactly how to do it. Before resorting to punishment, concentrate on teaching the lesson more clearly.

Punishment used judiciously is a valuable training tool, but ill-timed, inappropriate, or excessive punishment will make matters worse. Punishment should never be harsh enough to hurt or frighten your dog. In fact, pain confuses a dog and makes it almost impossible to think of anything but fight or flight.

House Soiling

House soiling can occur for a number of reasons, but the most common are lack of understanding and lack of physical control. Clean elimination cannot take place before a dog understands where he is supposed to relieve himself and how he is supposed to get there. A dog must be in good health and physically mature enough to control elimination until he reaches the proper area. Basic house-training is covered on pages 15 to 17; here we address only persistent problems.

Young Pups

Inappropriate elimination is most common in young pups, because of their immaturity. Patience and vigilance are the keys to success, so keep your young Lab pup confined to an area with a waterproof floor, and limit access to the rest of your home. Never allow a puppy to roam your house on his own. A rarely used room may seem suitably remote that a pup may think it is the indoor relief yard.

1. Take a pup under four months to his elimination area at least every two hours; during the first two months pups may need even more frequent outings.
2. Watch while the puppy voids and praise calmly when he finishes.
3. If an accident occurs, take the pup and a paper towel to the scene. Show him his mistake, then take the mess and the pup to the proper elimination area, scent the ground with it, and quietly praise your dog. *Never* push Buddy's nose into the mess; he would not understand and it's cruel.

Teach Buddy how to tell you when he needs to go out. Hang a bell on a string from the handle of the door leading to Buddy's elimination place. Each time you take him outside to relieve himself, ring the bell before opening the door. Most pups quickly realize that the bell has something to do with the door opening. Within a week or two, Buddy will try ringing the bell when he wants out—be listening!

Adolescent and Adult Dogs

Problems with house soiling by dogs over six months often result from improper early training, but may sometimes indicate health problems. If Buddy was formerly clean but has started soiling, something is wrong. Take him to the veterinarian right away for a health exam and urine and fecal tests. Infections, irritations, and parasites are common causes of elimination problems.

If Buddy scores a clean bill of health, then you should treat elimination problems as behavioral issues. Start Buddy's house-training over again with the techniques described for pups, even if he is mature. An adult dog can normally control his eliminative functions better than a pup, so outings will be less urgent but the training concept is the same.

Senior Dogs

A dog's golden years can be made miserable by incontinence. When age-related elimination problems occur, formerly clean dogs can become embarrassed and depressed by their lack of control. *Never* punish an older dog for incontinence—that would be cruel and, of course, would do no good.

Take your senior dog for a health check if he begins to be incontinent. He may have a health problem that your veterinarian can diagnose and treat.

Some spayed females develop urinary incontinence related to hormone imbalance. This problem may be distressing when first discovered but can usually be helped with a combination of medicine and more frequent outings.

A doggie diaper garment, available at many pet supply outlets, can be a useful and practical solution for incontinence in both males and females. The female diaper garment fits like panties, and the male style is a wide band that fastens around his loin area. Prolonged contact with urine can cause skin sores, so check the diaper garment and the dog's bedding several times a day and change it whenever it's damp.

Marking Problems

Canines, especially intact males, mark their territory with urine and feces. This works fine for wolves and coyotes, but when pet dogs mark, it may cause their owners distress, especially if they mark indoors.

Walk Buddy on leash twice a day to several outdoor spots and encourage him to mark there. Praise when he does. Dogs like to renew their marks frequently, so give Buddy the opportunity to do so.

Make certain Buddy has a chance every day to mark approved areas outdoors. Let him claim his turf by leaving messages on lampposts, rocks, or hydrants, but stop him immediately if he starts to mark stairs or porch corners. If he learns it's okay to mark the outside of your house, he may start claiming the furnishings too.

If Buddy's indoor marking has been going on for a few weeks or longer, it may take a while to stop him. Rather than letting him roam your house at will, keep him leashed to your belt so he can't try anything naughty without being noticed. Crate him at night to prevent midnight marking. Maintain this for three months so the dirty marking habit has time to fade and clean behavior strengthens.

A diaper garment can be useful for discouraging marking. When the dog attempts to mark, he'll only wet himself. Check the garment often for wetness and change it when it's damp.

Perhaps Buddy has no marking problems but you'd prefer that he not wet a particular shrub or garden statue.

1. Place a large rock or drive a stake into the ground as a new marking target for Buddy about a foot (30 cm) from the spot you wish to change.
2. Take him for a walk on lead to another marking spot and blot up some of his urine with a paper towel. Wipe the scented towel on the new marking target, then let him sniff there and mark.

With your guidance he will form the habit of marking the new spot and will neglect the old one. This trick also works on camping trips; place invitational marking targets a couple of feet away from your tent so Buddy will mark those instead of your shelter.

Nuisance Behaviors

Young Labs can be pretty rowdy. This is normal and can make for some good times, but some Labs are so boisterous they can be unpleasant to be around. Rowdy behavior often results from insufficient training and exercise, so work with Buddy daily on obedience lessons and be sure he also gets an hour or two of vigorous exercise. His manners will improve and his energy will be manageable.

Jumping Up on People

Dogs jump in greeting or play, which is fine in canine company, but most humans prefer not to be greeted by muddy paws. Jumping up on people, which may be cute when pups are small, becomes much less so as they grow. To avoid problems, don't allow Buddy to jump up, even while he is small.

Some people try to teach *No jump* by punishing the dog. This by itself seldom works. Instead, teach Buddy to sit politely when greeting you or another person. A treat reward and a loving touch will make this lesson pleasant. Good training in puppyhood will prevent a jumping habit, but adult dogs that jump can also learn to sit for petting.

Have Buddy sit every time he greets you. Don't pet him until he sits, and if he gets up, stop petting him. Teach family and guests to do this as well. Don't let any friends encourage your dog to jump on them or your good work will be undone.

For a confirmed jumping habit you will need to be more persistent than your Lab if you want him to quit.

Another no-jump lesson works when the dog is on one side of a gate (or door) and you're on the other, ready to open it. If Buddy jumps, simply wait until he tires of getting no response. When his feet are all on the ground, praise. Then ask him to sit. When he sits, praise again and open the gate.

These techniques work more reliably than punishment. Impoliteness is ignored and good manners are rewarded by the attention the dog desires. Dogs eagerly figure this out.

There are drawbacks to physical punishment for jumping. Traditional methods have injured many dogs and some handlers. Oddly, punishment is exciting to certain dogs. Rowdy dogs may interpret

Note: If Buddy nips hard or bites when he's jumping on people, get some hands-on help from an experienced professional trainer.

You can help your dog break the habit of jumping up on people.

pushing away as an invitation to play, to continue jumping, and to start nipping.

Chasing

The chase response is natural for dogs. Chase skills, vital for wild canines to catch food, have been modified by centuries of selective breeding into the herding and hunting drives of our modern dogs. This drive is important for much of the work dogs do for us, but can also lead to problems of chasing or nipping at moving objects or people.

Teach Buddy to ignore exciting movement by practicing a *sit-stay* or *down-stay* around moving objects. At first, Buddy may be so excited that he refuses to stay. Train him on leash so he does not run after the distractions.

OVERCOMING BEHAVIOR PROBLEMS

Once Buddy realizes you will not allow him to chase from a *stay* position, start working on *heel* (see page 62). As a moving object goes by, continue walking with Buddy in the *heel* position. If he does not chase, praise and reward him. If he *does* chase, turn and walk quickly in the opposite direction. Buddy will feel a tug when he reaches the end of the lead and will be turned around to face you. Repeat this until he figures out that chasing is not allowed.

Mouthing and Nipping

Nipping usually starts as a rowdy game but can become a habit that is hard for a dog to quit. Teach Buddy from the beginning that you disapprove of play-biting. Every time he puts his mouth on you, say *"Ow!"* in a deep, serious voice. If Buddy persists, walk away from him and refuse to play for five or ten minutes. If he comes to you apologetically, have him sit, pet him gently, and speak calmly, but wait a while before playing again.

If Buddy nips or mouths friends or family members, teach them what to do. Children may need you to intervene on their behalf, as dogs may tend to treat young children as they would their fellow dogs. If friends or children play rowdy games with Buddy, stop them immediately. He must learn never to put his teeth on a person's body or clothing.

Excessive Barking

Dogs bark; that's their voice. They bark from loneliness, excitement, or boredom. They bark in aggression, fear, or play. Labs are usually only a medium-vocal breed, but too much barking can become a problem if left unchecked.

Determine the cause of excessive barking by observing your dog's behavior. When is he barking? Where is he when he barks? Which direction does he face when barking? What can be seen and heard from his favorite barking position? These are all important clues to solving the problem.

A dog that spends a great deal of time in a yard or kennel may bark for many reasons. Dogs are group-living animals that can suffer from loneliness just as humans can. An isolated dog is as miserable as a shipwrecked sailor. If you don't have the time to exercise, train, and play with your dog, he will spend his life waiting for attention you are unable to give. This will cause misery for you both. Consider rehoming your bored, unexercised dog with someone who can better meet his physical and emotional needs.

Teach Buddy polite house manners so he can be brought into the house with the rest of the family. That will solve his barking problem.

If Buddy lives with your family but barks when everyone is gone, examine the environment to find out what is stimulating his barking. People walking or working nearby, animals, traffic, and other sights and sounds may cause Buddy to think he should guard your home in your absence. If Buddy barks when left indoors alone, try closing the curtains and playing calming background music to shut out sounds and sights that stimulate alarm barking. If Buddy is outside while you are away, move his pen to a less exciting spot or obstruct his view of any excitement to substantially reduce barking.

Leaving one or more food-puzzle toys for Buddy to chew in your absence can be a tremendous help with barking and other loneliness and boredom-based behavior problems. These toys hold food and can keep a dog busy for hours, working at coaxing out tidbits (see pages 23 and 78). A food toy can relieve boredom, keep Buddy's mouth busy, and replace barking as his favorite leisure pastime.

Some dogs bark when let outside and will not stop when commanded. This habit can become maddening as Buddy barks and you yell for him to be quiet—again and again. To solve this dilemma, call Buddy indoors and reward him with a treat for coming, but don't let him out again for 20 minutes. Do this every time he barks more than three or four times in the yard. If he won't come when you call, you'll need to teach him.

Refusal to Come

The main reason dogs refuse to come when called is that "*Come*" usually means "*The fun is over.*" You can prevent this by calling Buddy several times a day just to give him a treat and a pat. Use the same command and tone as when you "really" call him and the word "*Come*" will gain positive meaning.

If Buddy habitually refuses to come, you must prevent this behavior while you teach him a better response. Not coming is a hard habit to break and can be deadly, so working to change it is extremely important. Keep him on leash or a long line whenever he is outside your

To solve a barking problem, you must first determine the cause.

fence so he has no opportunity to lapse into his old bad habit.

1. Begin by teaching Buddy to come for treats when he is on the long line. Reward with praise, petting, and treats.
2. If he refuses to come, take up the slack and walk calmly in the opposite direction, holding the long line.
3. When Buddy notices and follows, stop and let him come up to you, then praise and give a treat. If he ignores you, he will feel the elastic action of the long line turn him partially around to face you. At this point, call again, as though nothing had happened.
4. Back away, coaxing Buddy to follow. Reel in the long line as he comes closer. When he's close enough to touch, gently but firmly take hold of his collar and then give him the treat reward.

Practice *come* on the long line at least four days a week in different locations and with varied distractions. Don't let Buddy run free for three whole months, even if he seems reliable on the long line. It will take time for the training to sink in.

After three months of long-line recalls, try it off lead in safe places. Continue training at least four times a week to keep Buddy in practice. Any time he refuses to come, use the long line for at least three days before allowing him to run free again.

> **Note:** Do not show the treat to Buddy to entice him to come; instead, hide the treat and produce it from your pocket or hand only when he sits obediently in front of you. If you make a habit of bribing Buddy to come by showing him a treat first, he may refuse to come if he doesn't see a treat or if the treat you show him doesn't appeal to him at that moment.

Begging

The average Lab is an optimist and likes to eat. These two natural traits, if misdirected, can combine to produce a terrible beggar. Prevent this by never, *ever*, feeding Buddy from the table. If you want to share your leftovers, put them in Buddy's bowl at his regular meal or, better yet, use them as training treats. Once a begging habit starts, the only cure is to never again feed tidbits from the table. Make sure family members and dinner guests follow this rule.

If Buddy is too interested in what's on your dinner plate, have him hold a *down-stay* beside your chair while you eat. That way, any drool will drip on the floor, not your lap. Also, from down there Buddy cannot see your food and will eventually tire of staring upward without reward.

Teach *come* by backing away and coaxing your dog to follow.

Stealing

Dogs are opportunists. If nobody is guarding what a dog wants, he will usually just take it. Until Buddy learns otherwise, he'll think it's okay to play with or chew on your belongings when you are not using them.

When Buddy steals something, go to him and take it away—pretrain for this with Thank You/Take It, on page 80—then help him find something of his own instead and praise him for taking it.

Punishment is generally not very useful for curbing a stealing habit, because in dog society being in possession of an item makes it your own. Humans think that once something belongs to us, it's ours until we give, sell, or trade it away. This is very different from how dogs think. When a dog stops chewing a bone and walks away from it, that puts the bone up for grabs. If another dog walks in and takes that unguarded bone to his bed to chew, under "dog law" it's now his and no legal case can be made against him for stealing. Punishing a dog for what we'd consider stealing makes little sense to the dog. Management, not punishment, is the key to preventing or curing a dog's "stealing" habit.

Food stealing, or "counter surfing" is a popular habit for Labs. Again, good management is the best solution. Keep him out of the kitchen with a closed door or gate unless someone is there watching him. If he shows interest in something on the counter, call him away and get him busy doing something else. Teach Buddy to do tricks and perform obedience skills for food rewards. Give him food-puzzle toys to work on every day, especially when you're too busy to watch him or when he's home alone. If Buddy knows how to get goodies "honestly," he'll be less apt to pilfer from counters and trash cans.

Minimize temptations so Buddy doesn't get into the habit of taking things you haven't given him. Clear counters of food after meals, teach your kids to put their toys away, and keep a tight-fitting lid on the kitchen trash. If Buddy doesn't find anything worth stealing for three to six months, he'll quit looking for it.

Shredding and Trashing

Shredding and trashing are extensions of stealing, so deal with them in the same way. Even if Buddy is trashing furniture, the concept is the same. We can safely assume he would have dragged that sofa he's shredding to his den it if wasn't so heavy.

A dog that trashes the house or yard when left alone not only ruins things, but endangers himself. Prevent this by confining Buddy safely when you must leave him. The crate-den is good confinement if you leave for only a short time. For a longer absence, a pen or puppy-proofed room is better. Give Buddy an entertaining chew toy to focus his energy while confined.

House-wrecking habits may take three months of safe confinement to cure. Do daily obedience training practice to give Buddy mental exercise and be sure he gets plenty of physical exercise. A dog that must spend hours confined has to use his energy somehow. Give Buddy positive attention that engages his mind and body, and the trashing problem should fade away. As mentioned in the section on barking problems (see page 100), if an owner cannot spend enough time with his or her dog to satisfy the dog's natural needs, it would be a kindness to rehome him with someone who could.

Roaming

The best cure for roaming is a well-fenced yard. Labrador Retrievers are hunting dogs and, if nothing prevents them, will joyfully trek off to hunt on their own. Unneutered dogs have another reason to stray every time sex hormones issue their siren call. Neutering often substantially reduces a dog's drive to roam. To keep Buddy safe, fence or pen him securely on your own property so that you will always know where he is.

Digging

Dogs dig to bury treasures, catch mice, entertain and exercise themselves, and make comfortable spots to snooze. A little

digging may be okay, but most owners draw the line when their backyard starts to look like a mine field. Digging is natural and fun, and a difficult activity for a dog to give up. It is possible, however, to limit and guide Buddy's digging, making it harmless.

First, fill all of Buddy's old holes, putting a bit of his feces near the top and finishing off with dirt. Now start a "good hole" in a spot you can allow Buddy to dig. Loosen the dirt about 6 inches (15 cm) down, hide dog biscuits under the surface, and encourage Buddy to dig them out. Praise for digging in the "good hole." Once or twice a day for three weeks, accompany Buddy to the approved excavation and encourage him to "*Dig here! This is your good hole! Good dig.*" Praise and be cheerful. Soon the only hole in your yard will be the "good" one.

Aggression Problems

If Buddy behaves aggressively toward you or any other person, have your veterinarian examine him to be certain he's not in pain or other distress. If health problems can be ruled out, ask your veterinarian to refer you to an experienced trainer or behaviorist for assistance. Some aggression can be successfully eliminated through good training, but a few dogs are too aggressive for normal family life and may require rehoming. In extreme cases, euthanasia may be necessary. A professional trainer or behaviorist can help you determine the best action for your specific case.

To prevent damage and escape, give your Lab an approved place to dig.

14 *Canine Good Citizen Test*

The CGC Certification Program

In recent years dog owners have felt a tightening squeeze of anti-dog legislation. Restrictions have been set in place in city, state, and national parks, and stringent leash laws are a national norm. "No Dogs" signs proliferate, blocking access to former ball-fetching fields and swimming areas. Unfortunately, there are good reasons for this restrictive trend. Children are chased and bitten on their way to school. Packs of dogs harass wildlife, terrorize cats, and devastate livestock. Bad-smelling, germ-ridden dog waste fouls playgrounds and gardens. Loose dogs, doing whatever they please, cause problems. If we'd take an honest look at our own behavior, we dog owners might have to admit that, as a group, we could be more responsible.

It would help our public image if we could convince our fellow citizens that dogs can be polite, friendly, and clean. There is a way we can do this. The American Kennel Club offers a Canine Good Citizen Certification Program, which recognizes well-behaved dogs and responsible owners.

The CGC test is not a competition and does not require precision performance, just normal polite behavior. Purebreds and dogs of mixed ancestry are equally welcome to participate and earn certification.

Most dog clubs and professional trainers could tell you when upcoming Canine Good Citizen tests are scheduled in your area. Ask to observe a test without your dog. CGC evaluators have years of experience in obedience, conformation, or field training and are knowledgeable about dog behavior. Evaluators, aware of the negative public attitude about dogs, work to make it more positive.

CGC evaluations are held in a relaxed setting, and tests simulate everyday situations. Each of the ten parts of the test presents a realistic challenge for Buddy to demonstrate good manners. Friendly strangers approach and may pet him. Distracting sights and sounds and other dogs will pass close by. You'll exit the room for a short while, leaving Buddy with the evaluator. Canine Good Citizens take this in stride.

Responsible Dog Ownership

When CGC evaluators decide whether to pass a dog, they are asked to consider whether the dog is

CGC training is a good way to maintain a polite, friendly, and clean dog.

- one they would like to own,
- safe with children,
- one they'd welcome as a neighbor,
- one that makes his owner happy while not making someone else unhappy.

Labrador Retrievers are known for their sunny disposition and delight in meeting new friends, but sometimes a vigorous Lab welcome can overwhelm people and leave a bad impression. If we'd like other people to appreciate our furry best friends, we must help our dogs control their boisterous good nature. Training for the CGC test is a good step in that direction.

Dog/handler teams successfully completing all portions of the test are awarded the Canine Good Citizen certificate. This program is steadily gathering public recognition. In 1991 Florida was the first state to pass a resolution supporting the CGC Program. As other states follow, the concept of responsible dog ownership gains more value and credence.

Canine Good Citizen certification means a dog is polite and under control in public. The more Buddy practices behaving properly, the more pleasant a companion he will become. You'll enjoy him more and so will other people. Also, Buddy's Canine Good Citizen certificate framed on your wall will be a proud reminder of the responsible relationship you've fostered with your lovable, well-behaved Lab.

Preparing for the CGC Test

Buddy should arrive for the test wearing a properly fitted buckle or slip collar of fabric, leather, or chain. Before testing, you will check in with the examiner, present a current rabies certificate, and proof of state or locally required licenses. Bring a brush or comb to be used on Buddy during test item three, and carry a plastic bag or other poop-scooping device, although, ideally, you won't need it during the actual test, as relieving himself during the test disqualifies a dog.

Ten Exercises That Make Up the CGC Test

The ten-part Canine Good Citizen test uses the basic *sit*, *down*, *stay*, *come*, and *heel* commands. This program encourages dogs and owners to cooperate and have fun together, so you are allowed to talk to and touch your dog to help him succeed. Praise and communication are emphasized, and no harsh commands or rough corrections are permitted.

You will need someone to help you practice for the CGC test. A family member or friend will do well at first, but to prepare for evaluation you'll need someone less familiar to Buddy. Professional dog trainers and most obedience clubs offer courses to help handlers prepare for the CGC test.

Test 1: Accepting a Friendly Stranger

The evaluator will approach and ignore Buddy as he or she talks and shakes hands with you. Buddy should sit politely beside you and must neither approach nor avoid the examiner.

Test 2: Sitting for Petting

The evaluator asks, "May I pet your dog?" and then pets Buddy while he sits or stands. Shyness, resentment, or jumping up are not acceptable. The dog may move, but must not be hard to pet.

Training for Tests 1 and 2: A cautious dog learns easier if first trained to stay while a friendly stranger talks to the handler and ignores the dog (Test 1). A cautious dog feels more secure when the stranger pets him if he has watched his handler be friendly with that stranger. If Buddy is neutral toward strangers or does not enjoy people, train for Test 1 first. Most Labs, however, are friendly and think strangers all want to be new friends. Their hardest challenge is waiting to be petted. This type may do best if you train for Test 2 (Sit for Petting) first. If you start training for Test 1 (Accepting a

Friendly Stranger), overfriendly Buddy may get frustrated having to wait through the whole people-only greeting before the petting happens. It's more rewarding and less frustrating for a very friendly dog to practice holding still for petting first, build his patience, then have him learn to wait while the friendly stranger greets you first.

1. Begin training by *heeling* Buddy up to your helper. Stop, *sit* Buddy, and tell him to stay. If he gets up, calmly reposition him and remind him to stay. Have your helper—let's call her Jane—keep her hands at her sides until Buddy will stay. You can command him to either sit or stand, but he must hold that position, then have Jane pet Buddy. Remind him to stay and praise when he does.

2. When Buddy has held the *stay* for petting three times in a row, he's ready for the next step. *Heel* him to Jane and command him to *sit* and *stay*, as before. This time, instead of petting Buddy, Jane shakes hands with you. Buddy may be surprised and disappointed that his new friend is greeting you first, and you may need to reposition him several times or start over. Stay calm; if *you* get flustered, so will Buddy. When Buddy will stay while you and Jane shake hands, then have her pet him. That's the reward Buddy has been waiting for so politely.

3. Instead of approaching Jane, have her approach you. Have Buddy stay while your helper walks up, greets you, shakes your hand, then inquires if she may pet your dog. Tell her she may, then remind Buddy to stay.

Test 3: Appearance and Grooming

The evaluator will examine Buddy, checking to see that he's clean and in proper condition. Then she will gently brush or comb him, using the tool you should bring to the test for this purpose. The evaluator will gently handle the dog's front feet and lightly examine his ears. Buddy does not have to hold a specified position for this examination, but he must not fuss. You may talk to him and praise and encourage him, but not restrain him in any way.

This test shows that Buddy will allow someone other than you to care for him. This is important for veterinarians, groomers, pet-sitters, and others you entrust with your dog.

Training for Test 3: The best way to train for Test 3 is by grooming Buddy often so that he enjoys it and looks forward to it. A short daily session with a fine-toothed comb will remove pesky fleas before they get established, and a weekly bristle brushing sweeps away dust, dander, and loose hair. A monthly bath will keep Buddy shiny and company-clean. Good grooming is pleasant for a dog; it makes him nicer to be near and demonstrates responsible ownership.

Test 4: Out for a Walk (On a Loose Leash)

Buddy may walk on your left or right during this test. You'll be directed to make a left turn, right turn, about turn, and stop at least once along the way and again at the end of the exercise. Command Buddy in a normal voice and encourage him along the way. He may sit at the halts, but this is not required.

Training for Test 4: This test shows that Buddy can walk politely at your pace. To train, practice walking Buddy on a loose leash, making stops, turns, and speed changes. Start training with few distractions, then work in more stimulating environments as Buddy's concentration improves.

Test 5: Walking Through a Crowd

In this on-lead test Buddy will walk close by three or more people and possibly another well-behaved dog. You may encourage and praise your dog and it's okay for him to show interest in the crowd, but he must not act fearful, pull at the leash, or sniff excessively.

Buddy should walk at heel or near your side, pay attention to you, and not interfere with passersby.

Training for Test 5: Train for this test by adding busier sidewalks to your walking practice.

Test 6: Sit and Down on Command/Staying in Place

To pass this exercise Buddy must sit and lie down on command and be able to stay until you release him. This test is per-

A Canine Good Citizen is polite and under control around strong distractions.

formed on a 20-foot (6.1-m) line in place of the regular leash. You may command more than once, and you may guide Buddy gently, but not push or pull him into position. A reasonable time is permitted and precision is not required, just polite obedience.

Training for Test 6:

1. Train Buddy to do Puppy Pushups (*sit*, *down*, *sit*, *down*), page 65, for treat rewards.
2. Every few pushups, give a *stay* command, step away for a moment, then step back and praise without allowing Buddy to change position.

Then turn, face him, and call. You may command more than once and encourage with voice and movement. Buddy must come close enough to be petted.

Training for Test 7: Practice with mild distractions first, adding stronger ones as Buddy's concentration improves. An occasional treat reward will make him more eager to come when called. You will not be allowed to carry or use treats during the actual test, but treat rewards will help you teach Buddy to come happily and promptly when you call him.

Test 8: Reaction to Another Dog

You and Buddy will approach another handler and leashed dog from a distance of about 30 feet (9 m). Stop and shake hands, chat, then continue on for 15 feet (4.6 m) or so. Buddy is allowed to show interest but not approach the other handler or dog, and he must not behave aggressively toward them.

Training for Test 8:

1. Start training Buddy on a *sit-stay* while a dog and handler approach and pass by without stopping. When Buddy can do this, have the handler and dog stop about 10 feet (3 m) away, facing you. With each success, have the handler stop closer until you are within hand-shaking distance. Dogs remain at *heel* while handlers interact.

2. When both dogs are comfortable with this, you and Buddy approach the

Dogs are allowed to show interest but not to approach the other handler or dog.

3. Wait a few seconds while he remains still, then give a treat. Gradually increase the distance to 20 feet (6.1 m) and build the amount of time he waits for the reward.

Test 7: Coming When Called

Your dog must come when you call from about 10 feet (3 m) away. You can tell Buddy to stay, or just let the evaluator pet him to distract him as you walk away.

other dog and handler while they remain still. Step by step, go through the same procedure as above until both dogs are comfortable.

3. Next, both handlers should approach each other with dogs at *heel* and pass without stopping, then stop 10 feet (3 m) apart, facing each other. With each approach, stop closer until you can walk up, halt, and your dogs will sit.

4. When you can do this, shake hands, and congratulate each other on your well-behaved dogs!

Test 9: Reactions to Distractions

This tests the dog's steadiness and confidence. Evaluators select two distractions involving sight and/or sound. Visual distractions may be a jogger, a bicyclist, or someone using crutches, a wheelchair, or a walker. The dog must not react with overexcitement, fear, or aggression. Auditory distractions may include knocking over a chair, dropping a book, or opening and closing a door. Dogs may show interest but not overreact.

Training for Test 9: Most dogs are curious about unusual sights, though some are wary until they know what the strange new thing is, and most dogs will startle momentarily when they hear a sudden loud noise. These reactions are okay, as long as the dog does not overreact by trying to escape or by defending himself. (See section on fears for advice on this.)

To train for this test, practice Buddy's obedience skills, especially *stays* and *heeling*, where there are unusual or exciting sights and sounds. Buddy will naturally be distracted at first, but should settle down after a few minutes if you keep working him and stay calm. If there are particular distractions that really steal Buddy's attention, work at a greater distance from these at first and gradually move closer. Some handlers try to avoid distractions while training, but that is a mistake. It's better to include normal distractions so Buddy learns to ignore them.

Test 10: Supervised Separation

This test shows that Buddy can stay calm when briefly separated from you. The evaluator will ask, "Would you like me to watch your dog?" and then hold Buddy's leash while you go out of sight for three minutes. The dog may move around a little but must not continually bark, whine, pace, or strain at the leash.

Training for Test 10:

1. Teach this by leaving Buddy with a helper and walking 20 feet (6.1 m) away. Stand there without looking at Buddy. After one minute return and praise him.

2. The next time go around the corner and wait a minute before returning. Gradually increase the time you're out of sight to five minutes.

3. After mastering five minutes, Buddy should easily pass the three-minute test required for CGC certification.

CGC Programs in Other Countries

By 2008, the United States Senate and thirty-five individual states had passed resolutions or proclamations in favor of the AKC Canine Good Citizen Test and its demonstrated positive effects on dog behavior, owner responsibility, and public safety. Canine Good Citizen programs are finding acceptance around the globe; Great Britain, Australia, Japan, Canada, Hungary, Denmark, and a growing number of other countries have developed their own variations of the AKC's program.

In the United Kingdom, the Good Citizen Dog Scheme test approved by The Kennel Club requires that a poop-scooping device be carried by the handler and a detailed ID tag be attached to the dog's collar. The test format is similar to that of the AKC, but dog and handler are also required to pass through a doorway or gate together as part of the *heeling* pattern.

In Australia, the New South Wales Good Citizen Assessment permits a broader variety of "appropriate collars or restraints," including head halters, harnesses, and gentle training collars. The test requires handlers to bring plastic bags, proof that they are ready for responsible dog waste disposal. The N.S.W. Assessment begins with the dog in a car, holding a *stay* position while the owner opens the door and attaches a leash to the dog's collar. On command, the dog exits the car, then sits and stays until the owner shuts the car door and gives a release command. If every dog owner enforced this rule, we could be certain of fewer road tragedies.

Canine Good Citizen certification is also gaining popularity among dog owners in Japan. Certain public areas formerly reserved for humans only now allow access to certified Canine Good Citizens. This adds greatly to owner motivation for certification and may result in more dogs receiving formal training.

Canine Good Citizen programs and their offshoots will undoubtedly have far-reaching effects that will ultimately benefit everyone.

Caninie Good Citizen programs will ultimately benefit everyone.

15 *Competition and Titles*

Overview

There is growing interest in competitions that demonstrate various aspects of canine beauty, brains, and brawn. Events are held and titles conferred by several organizations. Lab owners may find that their versatile dogs can earn titles in more than one event.

Each breed was developed to serve a particular purpose. A well-bred dog should inherit the temperament and physical capacity needed for his ancestral work. Conformation and performance events are opportunities for a dog to prove he has the qualities of body and mind representative of his breed.

Labs were developed as hardy water retrievers that could work under harsh conditions, yet keep a happy outlook. A Lab with a correct body should be able to run, swim, and retrieve. One with correct temperament should be readily trainable and work with enthusiasm.

Training and conditioning are important for a dog to do well in any competitive event. To be sure Buddy is sound and fit to withstand the rigors of training, have the veterinarian give him a complete checkup before launching his competitive career. Then seek out a training instructor with experience in the type of competition you're interested in and get started.

Conformation

Conformation events are known as dog shows. The purpose of dog shows is to sort out the best dogs to breed to produce the next generation. Spayed bitches and neutered dogs are not eligible for conformation competition.

Dogs are evaluated on how closely they conform to the official Breed Standards, which describe the proper conformation (body build and physical appearance) and correct temperment for each breed. The Standard for the Labrador Retriever is published in the *AKC Complete Dog Book*, and is also available from the Labrador Retriever Club of America (see pages 143–145 for addresses). Each breed is judged separately, then breed winners are judged together in seven designated groups. Labradors are in the Sporting Group. Dogs placing first in each group are judged together for Best in Show.

As they win, dogs earn championship points. Points earned are based on the number of dogs defeated. A maximum of five points can be earned at one show.

Home Schooling

Competing

To compete in conformation, Buddy must learn to gait in a straight line, pose in a balanced stance, and allow a thorough examination—including teeth and genitals—by a complete stranger—the judge. Shows are held both indoors and out, so Buddy must move confidently on both natural ground and rubber matting.

Bait is used to pose the dog and hold his attention in the conformation ring. It should be something the dog really likes. Many handlers use cooked liver or other enticing food. Some use squeaky toys instead of, or in addition to, food.

1. Teach your show prospect to bait by luring him to stand attentively for a tidbit, giving him small pieces as rewards. Encourage him to stand still and watch the bait for a moment, then give him a taste. Gradually increase the time he watches the bait before you reward him. Work on this for only a few minutes a day; don't bore him with unnecessary repetition.

2. While Buddy stands, move your bait a little to one side, then to the other. As he watches the bait, he will shift his weight and may move his feet slightly. Watch how this works and experiment a little; you can bait to move Buddy very slightly so he places his front feet evenly.

3. Once his front feet are lined up, keep his mind on the bait while you gently set each hind foot by hand, for a square stance.

At shows you will gait Buddy toward and away from the judge while he or she observes his movement. If Buddy will not move in a straight line, he will be difficult to evaluate and will probably not win. Practice walking and trotting him in a perfectly straight line. Use tape or chalk to make a visible line at first; later, just pick a point in the distance and move toward it.

Buddy can quickly learn to gait and pose, but be certain the patterns and positions you teach him are correct for show. Books and tapes are good study aids, but it takes hands-on coaching and practice to really learn to present a dog for judging. Most allbreed and specialty clubs offer conformation handling classes. With experts to guide you and a showlike setting to practice skills, a good handling class is invaluable to prepare for the ring.

Lure him to stand attentively for a tidbit.

Conformation showing displays a dog's soundness, type, and beauty.

To become a champion, a dog must earn fifteen points, including two major wins of three to five points under different judges.

Study the Labrador Retriever Standard before purchasing a dog to show. Educate yourself by reading, going to shows, and asking questions of experts, then buy the best pup you can from an experienced, successful show breeder whose dogs you admire. If Buddy comes from a long line of champions, he should inherit correct conformation. You may exhibit him yourself or have someone else handle him, but unless Buddy conforms to the breed Standard, the fanciest handling won't make him a winner.

Obedience Trials, Tests, and Titles

All breeds, including Labs, are eligible for Obedience trials. To compete, the dog must be registered with the sponsoring organization (AKC or UKC). Unlike conformation, neutered dogs are permitted in Obedience trials. If Buddy is purebred but not registered, and is neutered, he may be eligible for the American Kennel Club Purebred Alternative Listing (PAL/ILP), which will allow him to compete in performance events such as Obedience and Agility.

The purpose of Obedience trials is to demonstrate a dog's ability to obey under

Retrieving the dumbbell over a jump in Obedience competition.

The Open class, which leads to the Companion Dog Excellent (CDX) title, is the next step in Obedience competition. This level requires Buddy to heel free—including a figure 8—drop on recall, jump a broad jump, and retrieve on the flat and over a high jump. The group exercises require dogs to *sit-stay* for three minutes and *down-stay* for five while their handlers are hidden from view.

The Utility class requires a higher level of Obedience. Here Buddy can earn the Utility Dog (UD) title. Competitors demonstrate signal exercises, scent discrimination, directed retrieve, directed jumping, and the moving stand for examination.

After a dog has earned his UD he may be awarded the Utility Dog Excellent (UDX) title by earning qualifying scores in both Open and Utility at ten trials. Beyond that is Obedience Trial Champion (OTCh.). To be awarded the OTCh. title a dog must have a UD, earn 100 points, based on dogs he defeats in competition, and earn three first-place wins awarded by three different judges, one each in Utility and Open, plus another from either class.

To ready Buddy for Obedience competition, train around lots of distractions. To ready yourself, read and reread the regulations. To improve your teamwork, enter Obedience practice matches so you can work under realistic conditions.

distracting conditions. This shows his suitability as a companion. Dogs must demonstrate *heel*, *sit*, *stay*, *down*, *come*, and other skills.

Competition is at levels from Novice through Utility, each with increasingly complicated exercises. Entries in a class are all required to do the same exercises in order for the quality of their performances to be objectively measured.

Novice exercises differ slightly from AKC to UKC, but require dogs to heel through a series of turns on and off leash, perform a figure 8 around two people, stand for examination, come when called (the recall), and do *stays* as a group.

Rally

In Rally, handlers heel with their dogs through a course of numbered stations. At each station is a printed sign naming the exercise the handler and dog must perform. The exercises include many of the same skills performed in Obedience, plus others. The judge maps a course consisting of ten to twenty exercises selected from a set of about fifty. The exercises include left and right turns (90, 180, 270, and 360 degrees), pace changes, side steps, *sit, stand, down, stay,* call front, left and right finishes, pivots, serpentines, spirals, figure-8s, jumps, and more.

There are three titling levels in AKC Rally—Novice (RN), Advanced (RA), and Excellent (RE). A further title, Rally Advanced Excellent (RAE), can be earned after the RE title by qualifying in both the Advanced and Excellent classes on the same day and doing that at ten separate trials.

Novice Rally is performed on leash and the courses have signs from only the Novice set of exercises. Advanced is performed off leash and courses contain some Novice signs plus several additional Advanced exercises. Excellent is off leash except for the Honor exercise (a *sit* or *down-stay* with the handler holding the leash while the next dog runs the course.) Excellent courses include Novice, Advanced, and Excellent signs. Dogs must enter and leave the ring on leash at all levels.

In Obedience, the judge directs the handler around the course, but in Rally, the judge says only when to start and then the handler proceeds from station to station, following the numbers and performing each exercise in turn. Rally handlers learn and train for all the exercises, but only the judge knows which exercises will be used and the order in which they'll be performed on any specific day. A map of the course is made available to handlers about an hour before their class is called, and they are permitted a walk-through on the course, without their dogs, for ten minutes before judging begins.

A perfect score in AKC Rally is 100. A score of 70 or more is required to qualify (Q). Each handler/dog team starts with a perfect score and then points are deducted for performance errors committed by either the dog or handler. Point deductions may range from –1 for minor errors such as a crooked sit, a momentarily tight leash, or out-of-position heeling, up to –10 for performing a sign incorrectly. Handlers are allowed one retry per station if they think they've made a major error performing the exercise. Each retry costs 3 points off the score. Skipping a sign, having a consistently tight leash, and a few other faults are serious enough to result in a non-qualifying score (NQ).

Nearly unlimited verbal communication is allowed and encouraged in Rally, including multiple commands, praise and cheerleading, kissy sounds, or any other positive input from the handler to the dog. In Novice and Advanced, handlers are also permitted to clap their hands or pat their leg to get their dogs' attention, but those aids are penalized at the Excellent level. Handlers are not permitted to whistle, harshly command, touch, or correct/punish their dogs.

To train Buddy for Rally, work on brisk, attentive heeling. Heeling is the mainstay of Rally, and good, smooth, happy teamwork with your dog is important for success. Practice turns and pace changes while keeping Buddy in heel position. Teach him to come in straight to the front position (sitting close in front of you, facing you), and practice both the left and right finishes.

Keep Rally fun and fresh for your Lab—reward liberally with both praise and treats and don't practice for too long at a stretch. A Rally trial is an exciting event, working with many dogs and people moving and making noise near the ring. When Buddy is able to give you good, attentive heeling when you're training in a relatively quiet area, start practicing in gradually busier environments so he'll get used to staying focused on you, even in the midst of many distractions.

Tracking

Tracking is natural for Labs because of their excellent sense of smell. With training and practice, Buddy's natural skills can be fine-tuned and he may be able to earn a Tracking title.

There are three different Tracking tests, each more challenging than the preceding one. A dog need pass a test only once to earn a title. The titles are

1. Tracking Dog (TD),
2. Tracking Dog Excellent (TDX), and
3. Variable Surface Tracking (VST).

If a dog passes all three tests, he is awarded the Champion Tracker (CT) title.

Tracks are laid with several turns, and the dog must follow the scent with his nose close to the ground. Tracking dogs normally wear a harness and are encouraged to lean their weight into it when following a trail. The handler can feel the dog's confidence on the scent through the taut lead.

Scent is invisible, yet a dog can follow it as if it were a neon path. When a person walks across a field, a scent trail is left behind, consisting of microscopic cells that constantly slough from our bodies. Each person's chemical makeup is different, so everyone leaves a unique trail. A dog can detect the difference by scent.

Scent is carried by air currents but flows like water. It pours over and around objects, leaving traces behind. It settles in low places, clings more to soft surfaces than hard, and remains longer in sheltered areas than in exposed ones. A handler must learn to read the dog's subtle cues to know when to encourage him and when to slow down.

1. To start Buddy tracking, just hide and let him find you. In the beginning, move away from him in a straight line and just barely conceal yourself at the end of the track. Make it easy at first, adding difficulty as his skill grows.
2. When he grasps the concept of finding you, teach Buddy to find someone else. Have your helper scuff the ground to make a highly scented starting patch, then walk away and hide out of view. Wait a few minutes, then show Buddy the scuffed spot and encourage him to follow the scent trail leading to your helper's hiding place. When he finds the helper, both of you should praise and reward him.
3. As Buddy catches on, add a 90-degree turn, then another, as proficiency grows. Let the trail age ten minutes before following, then a half hour, then longer. Add more turns and time to make the trail more challenging as Buddy becomes skilled.

Field trials keep dog and handler functioning as a hunting team year-round.

Opinions differ on the use of food in training for tracking. Some trainers swear by it, smearing crushed frankfurters or cheese on the soles of the tracklayer's shoes to keep a new dog's nose deep in the footsteps. Some place bait at the turns to encourage a dog to keep going. Other trainers claim that food distracts a dog's nose and never use it at all. Experiment to find what works best for Buddy.

Field Trials—Hunting and Retrieving

Retriever field trials and hunting tests present opportunities to demonstrate the usefulness of well-trained retrievers. These events provide activities that keep a dog and handler functioning as a hunting team year-round. Field events are meeting grounds for bird hunters and dog breeders, and proving grounds for breeding stock. Labs can perform on both land and water and do well in both retriever trials and noncompetitive hunting tests.

To start Buddy in field trialing, first teach basic obedience commands with voice, hand signals, and whistle cues. Buddy will need to listen and watch for directions because in some retrieves the dog must rely on his handler to send him toward a downed bird he cannot see.

Labs are natural retrievers, but a good bird dog must learn to properly fetch the bird. He must not drag it by the head or wing, but carry it by the body, deep in his mouth. The dog must have a gentle

mouth, never chomping down or playing with the bird as he brings it directly to you.

For water retrieves, Buddy must leap in vigorously, not wade out or hesitate on the bank. Swimming comes easily to most Labs, but their introduction to water should be made as pleasant as possible. Never throw a dog in to teach him to swim; that will diminish both his fondness for water and his trust.

There are a number of books available that are completely devoted to training for retrieving work, and they may help you teach yourself (see Useful Addresses and Literature, page 142). However, nothing beats one-on-one coaching in the

The tire jump is part of an Agility trial.

field from an experienced trainer. Go to retriever trials and watch the experts work. You'll meet handlers with many years of experience who'll be glad to help a sincere newcomer.

Agility

Agility trials are exciting, fast-moving events in which dogs dash over jumps and across bridges, crawl through tunnels and tires, and thoroughly enjoy themselves. Agility trials are open to all breeds, although the faster, lighter dogs have a definite speed advantage over heavier ones.

Agility contestants perform using a series of obstacles that test the dogs' ability to jump, weave, run, and follow handlers' directions. Obstacles must be taken in the correct order and within a time limit. Events are scored on a time-plus-faults basis, with the winner being the dog with the lowest numerical score. Several organizations sponsor Agility trials and offer titles. Rules and regulations differ from group to group, but the basic idea is the same.

There are three levels in AKC Agility. At each level, to earn a title Buddy must qualify at three trials:

1. The Novice course has from 13 to 15 obstacles. The Novice Agility (NA) title is awarded to dogs that qualify at three trials.
2. Open Agility (OA) courses have from 16 to 18 obstacles.
3. At the Agility Excellent (AX) level there are from 18 to 20 obstacles. Many obstacles are jumps of various sorts.

The following are some of the obstacles you will encounter:

- **The dog walk:** An 8- to 12-foot (2.4- to 3.7-m) long elevated plank with inclined ramps at each end for entrance and exit.
- **Weave poles:** 6 to 12 upright poles in a row, with enough room for the dog to slalom between.
- **Open tunnel:** A flexible tube, open at both ends, that the dog runs through.
- **Closed tunnel:** A solid short tube the size of a 50-gallon (189-L) barrel, with a long cloth sleeve at the exit end; the dog must push his way through the collapsed sleeve.
- **Seesaw:** Similar to the type found in a playground.

- **Pause table:** A short-legged platform the dog hops onto, waits five seconds, then exits.
- **A-Frame:** Two 8- to 9-foot (2.4- to 2.7-m) panels hinged upright together like a roof; the dog ascends one side and descends the other.

Several types of jumps are used in Agility: single-, double-, and triple-bar jumps, panel jumps, window and tire jumps, and broad jumps. These can be adjusted to different settings, based on the dog's height. The lowest jump division is 8 inches (20 cm), for dogs 10 inches (25 cm) tall or less. The highest is 24 inches (61 cm), for dogs 22 inches (56 cm) or taller.

You can start training for Agility with homemade obstacles, but be careful that your obstacles are sturdy and safe before asking Buddy to try them.

Jumping is hard on a young dog's body, so avoid jumping Buddy until he passes his first birthday. Even then, let him build his strength gradually to avoid injuries. If Buddy is a sedentary adult, the same rule holds: Build up gradually. When a dog is having fun, he may not notice if something hurts, and even if he does, he may not admit it until afterward.

Good luck, and have fun in competition!

16 *Sports*

Avoiding Injuries

A wide choice of organized and individual physical activities are available for dogs and owners. Sports and games are fun, burn energy, build strong muscles, and often lead to friendships, but sports injuries can occur. This is true for both dogs and humans, so before starting a new sport, have the veterinarian check your dog and have your own physician examine you to be sure you're both sound and healthy.

Many sports injuries can be prevented by first warming up with a brisk walk before plunging into the game. Whichever sport you choose, be sure to practice regularly to stay in shape. If you and Buddy are couch potatoes all week and active only intermittently on weekends, you'll increase your chances for injury. During periods when you cannot practice your sport, be sure to keep both you and Buddy in good physical shape with a healthy daily exercise program.

Suggested Sports

Here are some sports and games that might appeal to both you and Buddy.

Flyball

If you like fast action and Buddy is wild for tennis balls, flyball may be your game. This is a team sport open to dogs of any breed. In fast-paced relays, each dog jumps four hurdles, then hits the pedal on a spring-loaded box that pops out a tennis ball. The dog catches the ball, then carries it back over the jumps to the start/finish line. Each dog on the team takes a lap—runs, jumps, hits the box, and races back with a ball. The team completing the round in the fastest time with fewest errors wins.

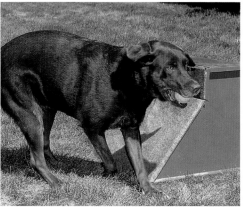

In Flyball, the dog hits the box that dispenses the ball.

All breeds are eligible under North American Flyball Association rules, and teams often consist of more than one breed. It's advantageous to have a little dog on a flyball team, as jump heights are set for the smallest member. Dogs participating in flyball must not be aggressive toward each other, even when greatly excited.

Flying Disk Catch

A popular way to exercise dogs is by throwing a flying disk for them to chase and catch. The disk sails farther with less arm exertion than a ball or stick, so it's easier on the handler. Some dogs enjoy playing with the disk so much that they carry one around most of the time, even napping with it as a pillow.

Regional and national contests are held for disk-catching dogs. One event includes timed throws, with points for catches and bonuses for aerial snags. Another event demonstrates the dog's athletic style. Some of the leaps and turns are astounding.

Disk catching can be fun and good exercise, but it can also be hazardous. Takeoffs require good muscle strength and coordination, which is an exercise benefit, but landings can be very rough on joints. Repeated jolts to legs can cause damage over time, particularly in heavy breeds like the Labrador Retriever, and can lead to permanent pain and stiffness. Also, a serious back injury can occur when a dog twists sharply in midair to catch the disk, causing permanent damage.

To have fun with the flying disk but avoid injuries, save disk catching until Buddy is fully grown and his joints and

Flying disk games are fun and provide good exercise, but excessive twisting and hard landings can injure a dog.

muscles are firm. Even then, don't throw high in the air; throw along the ground or just above your dog's head. That way Buddy will run fast and grab the disk as it goes by but not make those joint-wrecking leaps and twists. You can exercise Buddy to a pleasant state of tiredness without laming him.

Musical Freestyle Obedience

Freestyle is dancing—with dogs. This activity combines *heeling* and obedience exercises with elements derived from both equine dressage and pair figure skating. Freestyle builds coordination and improves flexibility while teaching a dog to be attentive to cues from his handler. All breeds are eligible for this rapidly growing sport. Pups as young as ten weeks or dogs in their silver years can train for freestyle.

Handlers set moves to music. Any type of music will work—march, waltz, swing, reggae, rock and roll—but it should suit your dog's natural rhythm and make you want to move your feet. Dogs heel attentively on either side, turn circles, and weave through or jump over the handler's legs. They walk forward, backward, and sideways, bow, shake a paw, sit, lie down, roll over, crawl, and stand still on signal. Handlers and dogs move together in rhythm. The combinations of moves possible in freestyle are myriad.

You and Buddy will both contribute your ideas to your freestyle routine. Sometimes the handler will ask for a practiced move, but the dog may come up with something different on his own. Unlike other canine performance sports, in freestyle it is okay to accept interesting behavior offers from the dog. Often the dog's idea improves upon that of the handler.

1. Begin freestyle training by focusing Buddy's attention on a food tidbit and starting to walk. What you do with your lure will govern Buddy's movement and position.

2. First work on smooth *heeling*; here is where the music comes in. Music has a beat that helps propel dog and handler forward together. You don't have to step to every beat, but do move with the music and let it move you. Use treat lures to guide your dog, reward-ing intermittently. At first, Buddy will just follow the lure, but as he does he will learn specific hand signals for various moves.

3. Reward with treats as you dance, always pairing them with a sound, like a click of your tongue or verbal "*Yes*" to mark correct behavior. Phase out treats as Buddy gains skill, using the marking sound to reward while dancing and saving tidbits for afterward. When freestyle teams perform in public, audiences show their approval with applause—better than treats.

Water Sports

Swimming is great fun for this breed. Labs are born for the water, but not every Lab is comfortable in water at first. Allow your dog to get used to being in water at his own pace. *Never* throw a dog in; he may panic and take in a lungful of water instead of air. With his smooth, water-repellent coat, webbed feet, and rudder-like "otter" tail, a trip to the lake or bay is a supreme treat for a Lab. Remember to dry out those pendulous ears after swimming, though, so fungus and bacteria don't move in. Many dogs will drink salt-water when thirsty, causing vomiting and further dehydration, so be sure to carry fresh drinking water when you take Buddy to ocean beaches.

Swimming is good exercise that's gentle on joints, so it's good for pups through seniors; however, don't overtire a pup or a sedentary dog with too much swimming all at once. Let Buddy build his strength and stamina gradually. Labs are such avid

Swimming is good exercise for pups through seniors.

water retrievers that it's hard to notice when the dog begins to tire. Exhaustion in deep water can be dangerous, so make Buddy rest on shore for a minute or two every few throws.

Boating can be enjoyable with a dog once he learns good manners afloat. Teach basic commands, especially *down* and *stay*, before inviting Buddy aboard. An overexcited dog can be a hazard, and the smaller your boat, the more important it is that your dog be calm and obedient.

If your boat is small and tends to tip easily, familiarize Buddy with the rocking motion in shallow water first. Have him sit or lie down and stay while you rock the boat. Praise him for staying. Repeat a few times, building gradually to heavier rocking. When Buddy is not bothered by the motion, you're ready for deeper water. For more on boating, see page 85.

Dock Jumping

In dock jumping sport, dogs leap from a dock into a pool, lake, or other body of water. The dock is usually 40 feet (12 m) long and 8 feet (2.4 m) wide, with the dock's end about 2 feet (60 cm) above the water. The dock is covered with a turflike carpet for better traction. The water is required to be at least 4 feet (1.2 m) deep. The dog's jump is measured from the end of the dock to the point where the base of the dog's tail breaks the water's surface. Prizes are awarded for the longest and highest leaps. The world's record jump length (as of January 2009) is 28 feet 10 inches (8.9 m), and the record vertical jump is 7 feet 10 inches (2.4 m).

Dogs six months or older, of any breed or mix, are welcome to compete in dock jumping. The dog's handler tells him when to jump from the dock. Handlers may optionally throw a toy only to motivate the dog to leap into the water, but the dog is required to retrieve the toy in the retrieval competition class. Each dog jumps twice, in round-robin order, with the better of the two jumps considered that dog's official measurement for that competition.

Dock jumping is becoming a worldwide sport, with events held in the United States, Great Britain, Japan, Australia, and Germany. Competitions are offered by DockDogs and by the United Kennel Club.

Additional Outdoor Activities

Hunting

Labs have earned a strong reputation as good all-around hunters and retrievers, but not every Lab has what it takes to work in the field, so if you plan to hunt, choose your dog from proven field stock.

Keep Buddy fit, year-round, with good diet, exercise, and grooming. The health and attitude of a hunting dog improves with daily attention and training. The stronger your bond of companionship with Buddy, the better he'll behave for you in the field.

A hunting dog must be steady on basic commands, following directions by voice, hand signals, and whistle. Dog and handler must function as a team to find and bring home game. A field dog must ignore distractions from other dogs, hunters, and nontarget game.

Basic obedience is a good start for teaching Buddy to obey commands and ignore distractions. After basic training he'll need to learn field skills. There are

books on field training available, but if you are inexperienced, consider sending Buddy to a professional field trainer. Professional lessons for both you and your dog would make you a better team.

Skijoring

If you like gliding on skis over fresh snow, consider skijoring with Buddy. This sport involves a skier being pulled by a harnessed dog—great winter fun for a muscular Lab. This can become a fun year-round activity if you teach Buddy to pull you on a scooter or in-line skates (being careful around traffic, of course). Dogs will run until exhausted if they're having fun, so it will be up to you to make sure Buddy doesn't overtire himself. Take rest breaks when you think he might need them, and be sure to carry drinking water for both of you.

A harness is used for pulling tasks, as it spreads the pressure across the broad chest area and does not obstruct the dog's breathing by pressing against his throat as a collar would. You will not have control of your dog with only a harness, however, so he should also wear a collar or head halter and a leash so you can turn and stop him.

Teach voice commands for *left*, *right*, and *whoa*. Enforce the commands with the leash by directing Buddy to the side you command or pulling back when you want him to stop. This part of the training should be done on dry ground, without skates or skis, by walking behind the dog as he pulls into the harness.

Running through snow is serious exertion, so let Buddy build up to this exercise gradually. Along the way, stop occasion-

Three-dog sled racing team.

ally to rest. Offer him frequent small drinks of water, rather than letting him get too thirsty and drink a lot at once. Check his paws for ice buildup between the pads, which can be very painful. Remove the ice gently; the webbing between toes is sensitive.

Mushing

If you like skijoring or other snow sports and have several Labs, you might consider teaching them to pull a dogsled as a team. There's no rule that sled dogs have to be traditional breeds such as Malamutes or Huskies. Labs love a good workout and can handle cold weather quite well.

Carting

If winter sports are not your pleasure and the idea of mushing through snow leaves you cold, you might consider carting instead. Teach Buddy to pull a dog-sized sulky or wagon for exercise and fun. As with skijoring, have him wear a collar or head halter for control as well as a pulling harness, and teach him voice commands to turn and stop. You and Buddy may draw a lot of attention in your neighborhood as you practice carting. Children are fascinated by dogs doing actual work, and may follow you around as you train, begging for rides. Buddy probably will love all the attention.

17 *Careers for Labs*

The Labrador Retriever's history of working for, and with, humankind began with the first of his breed and continues today. Labs are energetic, sociable, clever, versatile, hard workers. They are famous as hunting retrievers, of course, but also excel in other careers. A healthy, properly trained Labrador Retriever can do just about any job that dogs can do.

Assistance Dogs

Labs are strong, steady, energetic, and gentle. They take training seriously and have a fairly long life span. This makes them well suited as assistance dogs, and the Lab is among the breeds most favored for this. Several training schools have breeding programs to produce Labs with strong inherited ability for this work. Some assistance dog candidates are donated by breeders; others are from shelters.

Pups are usually placed after weaning with volunteer puppy raisers. The pups grow up in their foster homes, learning good manners, basic obedience, and social skills until they are mature enough for specialized training. At that point, they receive professional training, which culminates in placement as assistance dogs. Candidates not suited for assistance work

are placed with families as exceptionally well-educated companion dogs.

All dogs trained to help people with disabilities are known as assistance dogs. Several careers exist within this general classification:

Guide dogs were the first to receive public recognition. They assist blind people, leading them through crowds and across intersections, helping them to find doors and avoid obstacles. A guide dog must be obedient, yet so intelligent that he knows when to disobey a command that would place his blind partner in danger. This is a job that takes a very special dog.

Hearing dogs assist deaf people, alerting them to important sounds such as doorbells, a baby's cry, or someone calling the person's name. The presence of a hearing dog is more than a comfort; the dog can truly be a lifesaver, alerting his partner to fire alarms, sirens, and other important warning sounds.

Service dogs assist people with mobility problems, pull wheelchairs, open doors, turn lights on and off, and retrieve objects. These dogs wear backpacks, carrying their partner's supplies for the day. A service dog helps with daily chores. At the grocery store he places items into the shopping cart, then helps unload and put them away at home. He can do just about anything from pressing elevator buttons his partner cannot reach from a wheelchair, to fetching something from the refrigerator.

Seizure alert dogs are able to sense impending seizures and to warn their partners so that a safe spot can be reached before seizure activity begins. These dogs will block the partner's path to indicate a seizure is coming, not allowing the person to ignore the warning. During a seizure, he stays right there, usually in physical contact, watching over his partner. Afterward, he comforts his partner until things return to normal. With the seizure alert dog's help, a person can live a much freer life.

Assistance dogs allow people with disabilities much more independence than they would otherwise enjoy. The dogs go everywhere with their human partners— to work and school, and on social outings. The companionship and confidence an assistance dog brings his partner are beyond measure. There is no stronger bond between a person and a dog than that between an assistance dog and his partner.

Therapy Dogs

Therapy dogs are usually privately owned companion animals that regularly visit patients in hospitals and nursing facilities. The main job of a therapy dog is to share unconditional love and affection. A friendly Lab can do this well. Training Buddy as a therapy dog would be a rewarding way to share his love with others.

Guide dogs lead their blind partners through crowds and busy intersections.

To become a therapy dog, Buddy must be friendly and trusting, enjoy petting, and be neither aggressive nor fearful of strangers. He won't need precision obedience, but must walk politely on leash, sit, lie down, and stay when commanded.

A therapy dog must be socialized around all kinds of people and remain calm and confident in unpredictable situations that can occur while visiting. Therapy dogs may encounter unusual odors, sudden sounds, elevators, wheelchairs, and other things they may not experience at home. They must patiently tolerate not only gentle petting, but hugging, pinching, and fur pulling, and must not be overly concerned with people shouting or crying.

There are several organizations that register therapy dogs (see Useful Addresses

A Therapy Dog can help children learn.

and Literature, pages 144 and 145). Each has different requirements for registration, but most insist that the candidate pass skill and temperament reviews similar to the Canine Good Citizen test (see page 105). Some organizations use the AKC's CGC test to screen; others have devised their own.

Some health care facilities will allow only registered therapy dogs to visit; others don't require official registration. Check on this when you call for an appointment to visit. One advantage of registration is that members become eligible for special group insurance.

Search Dogs

Search dogs find people when human rescuers cannot. The dog's sense of smell is many hundreds of times more sensitive than our own. Our poor human noses can barely identify a best friend's cologne, whereas dogs can discern with just one whiff a person's gender, state of health, and if their car needs a tuneup!

The Lab's excellent scenting ability and love of games suits him well for search training. Although finding lost hikers or disaster victims is not sport to us, it is to the dog. Dogs enjoy scent skill challenges from an early age. Start nose games when Buddy is a pup and graduate to tougher finds as he matures.

A real search is not like a competitive tracking test. Real searches lead through unexpected hazards, and trails might be days old and cross roads, rivers, and animal tracks. Search dogs must find their footing on twisted rubble, avoiding sharp debris while seeking victims in collapsed buildings.

To train and perform search work, both dog and handler must be physically fit and able to function under stress. A search always includes the unexpected and not every search has a happy ending. Besides managing their dogs, search dog handlers must manage their own emotions. For the right type of person, however, search and rescue work with a dog can be one of the most rewarding jobs in the world.

Begin training Buddy as a pup, encouraging him to use his nose:

1. Hide a toy under a blanket and encourage him to find it.
2. When Buddy isn't watching, go hide and call him to find you.
3. Have a family member hide while you wait with Buddy; after a few minutes, go search together.

Make a big deal out of every find—praise, petting, treats, toys, whatever Buddy enjoys most. Finding objects and people by scent will become Buddy's favorite game.

Outdoor nose games are fun. A woodsy area with trees to hide behind is a great playground to practice on. Eventually, Buddy will be able to find you so easily it will be nearly impossible to hide from him. Sometimes have a friend hide, so Buddy can learn to find other people too.

Train your prospective search dog in obedience and Agility. He'll need good manners and self-control and should be able to climb under, over, around, and through all kinds of obstacles. If Buddy shows potential for search work, find a volunteer search and rescue group in your area. You'll meet experienced people who are very dedicated to this work and can help you fine-tune Buddy's—and your own—abilities.

Show Biz

So, you've trained Buddy in obedience, and he can do 27 tricks with hand signals only,

wear a T-shirt, hat, and sunglasses, and sing harmony to "Auld Lang Syne." What now? Maybe Hollywood or Broadway.

No kidding, there's work out there for canine talent. Buddy doesn't even need to be able to perform 27 tricks. What he does need, however, is a willing disposition, a good rapport with you, and a bit of that special, elusive presence that makes the stars shine. If that describes your Buddy, and the idea of seeing him on the stage or screen appeals to you, then consider show business.

Although starring roles are limited, there might be an upcoming show that needs a handsome, well-trained dog like Buddy. Another venue might be advertising. Dogs have an appeal that sells products and are often used in magazine and television ads. Dog foods, dog treats, and dog toys all use canine models, of course, but products unrelated to dogs also use canine charisma to attract customers.

To prepare Buddy for acting work, first teach him the basic commands *come*, *sit*, *down*, *stand*, and *stay*. He should also learn *go*, so you can send him to a designated spot without taking him there.

Once basics are mastered, start teaching tricks. Be imaginative! Why stop at *shake a paw* if you can also get a *high five*, *wave*, and *salute*. Why do boring *sit-stays* if Buddy can *sit-stay* on a chair while wearing a hat and holding a flag in his mouth. If *fetch-the-stick* is getting too easy, try *fetch-the-paper*, *fetch-the-chips*, or *fetch-the-slippers-and-pipe*. Take pictures of Buddy doing those things for his acting portfolio. At the very least, you'll create great home entertainment.

18 Legal Issues

Community Responsibility

Dog ownership, though usually in pursuit of happiness, is not a right specifically guaranteed by our Constitution. We may never discover how this slipped past the founding fathers, but until an amendment officially makes it a right, owning a dog is a privilege and a responsibility.

We share our communities with other citizens, some of whom do not appreciate dogs. Pro- and anti-dog factions are often at odds over the use of public recreation areas. Dog owners ask for off-leash exercise areas in the parks, non-dog neighbors want our critters banned from parks altogether. Reasons given to exclude dogs, on close examination, turn out to be people problems, such as rudeness and irresponsibility, rather than anything intrinsic to dogs.

Public parks are for people to share. Owners who permit their dogs to run amok through playgrounds, dot grassy lawns with feces, and chase wildlife make parks less enjoyable for the majority. It's sad to say, but the anti-dog argument points a righteous finger of blame. The solution is not to close the parks to dogs, but for us dog owners to take our responsibilities more seriously. We must teach our dogs polite manners, keep them from bothering

other park users, always clean up their messes, and remind other dog owners to do the same. If more owners did this, there would be fewer complaints from non-dog people and more off-leash areas where our dogs could be allowed to play.

Dog Waste Pickup and Disposal

Nobody likes dog waste. Some dog owners prefer not even to know where their dogs defecate, an attitude that is both foolish and selfish. Foolish, because a dog's health can be monitored by noting changes in his bowel movements. Unusual consistency, color, or odor all may warn of developing problems. Selfish, because if a dog isn't messing in his own yard, he must be messing in someone else's. This selfishness insults neighbors and makes the dog look like a slob when, really, the owner is.

In many places, leaving dog feces around violates the law. In some communities, failure to carry a poop-removal device when walking a dog in public carries a fine of $500 or more. Unfortunately, most communities fail to enforce these laws; if a few big fines were levied and local media ran the story, I think we'd see a sudden jump in cleanups. Since this has not happened, however, despite all the laws on the books, inconsiderate dog owners still leave their calling cards behind.

There is a way we, as responsible dog owners, can let the slobs know we notice their actions, or lack thereof. When you see one starting to leave the scene after his or her dog finishes his business, assertively offer one of the many plastic bags you carry, ready for action, in your coat pocket.

Some people will graciously thank you, take the bag, and pick up. Smile at this type of person and compliment his or her dog's appearance or manners. Be pleasant; by rewarding responsible dog owner behavior, you'll encourage it. The next time you see that person walking his or her dog, wave and say hello.

Owners who ignore their dog's mess may also try to ignore you when you point it out. If you offer a cleanup bag and the person continues to walk away from the scene, don't give up. Without becoming argumentative, offer the bag again, this time a bit louder—perhaps the person didn't hear you the first time. If that fails, use the bag yourself. Yes, go ahead and pick up the other dog's mess. At least that way nobody will step in it and mutter curses against all dogs and their owners, including you and your innocent Buddy.

Licensing and Local Laws

Before the license to drive a motor vehicle is granted, applicants must pass a test proving their knowledge of road rules. No such test exists for a dog license. It is the individual responsibility of each dog owner to know and abide by the laws that pertain to our companion animals.

Dog licensing laws exist in practically every community. Some dog owners complain that towns mandating dog licensing have no such requirements for gerbils, ferrets, or potbellied pigs, but whether or not one agrees with the policy, abiding by licensing laws is part of responsible dog ownership. The AKC agrees, and asks for proof of a current dog license—where locally required—to pass their Canine Good Citizen test.

Fairness to Neighbors—Fences

Although we may adore everything about our own dogs, our neighbors may not. Ill-mannered dogs are a major cause of neighborhood disputes. The most common problems are doggie trespassing and excessive barking, both of which infringe on peace and privacy. A good fence will keep Buddy home, safe, and out of trouble.

When the poet Robert Frost wrote "Mending Wall," he was referring to personal boundaries, not dog ownership issues. Nevertheless, his famous phrase "Good fences make good neighbors" does pertain to our furry friends. A good fence will prevent Buddy from trespassing and therefore foster more positive neighbor relations.

The cost of erecting a fence may seem high until you weigh it against the cost of repairing dog damage to your neighbor's property. Add a lawsuit over the playful dog knocking down a neighbor's child and the price of a fence looks like a bargain.

Most dogs can be trained to respect the boundaries of a fence.

Some dogs will honor a fence simply because it's there; others must be trained to do so. Before you leave Buddy in the fenced yard, walk him around the area on leash. If he jumps up on the fence or tries to push under it, pull him back and sternly tell him to "*Stay in the yard*," then praise him calmly for leaving the fence. The first time you turn Buddy into the fenced enclosure alone, watch for a while from a hidden location. Let Buddy explore and check the yard, but if he starts to test the fence, pop out and rush over to scold him for not respecting the boundary.

Check the fence and gates daily for a while to make sure Buddy is not working on an escape route. Fill any excavations you may find along the fence line with Buddy's excrement, topped off with a layer of clean soil. Most dogs will not dig through their own feces. If your dog does, however, you will need to secure your fence by trenching

all around and burying fence wire a foot or two (30 cm) deep, then attaching it to the above-ground fence.

Electric Fences for Inventive Escapers

For dogs that have perfected the art of escape, other steps must sometimes be taken. A very good cure for both climbing and digging is to add a strand of electric fence wire, such as the kind used for farm animals, to the top and bottom of your fence. Buddy will learn to stay home because the fence will zap him if he tries to get out.

To secure your yard with the electric fence, string a strand inside the existing fence, near top and bottom, using 6-inch (15-cm) plastic insulators designed for this purpose. You'll also need a power pack to energize the fence, available either in hard-hitting livestock variety or with a milder shock designed especially for pets. Either should do the job if you set up the situation correctly to start.

Before leaving Buddy alone in the yard, you must train him to not touch the fence. If he tries to escape and accidentally discovers that the shock is tolerable and lasts only a moment, he may ignore the discomfort and escape at will. Prevent this casual attitude by tricking him into touching the new wire with his nose or tongue. This might seem unfair, but it's vital to prevent escape.

Before you turn on the fence, twist strips of aluminum foil, 1 inch (2.5 cm) wide and 1 foot (30 cm) long, onto the wire every 50 feet (15 m) or so, letting the ends dangle free so Buddy will notice them. Bait these shiny "flags" by smearing them with cheese or liverwurst to tempt him to touch them. If Buddy's first experience with the fence is very unpleasant when he sniffs or licks a hot flag, he will avoid future contact.

Electronic Containment Systems

With this type of system the dog wears a collar that receives electronic impulses from a transmitter wire that can be installed either above or below the ground. When the dog approaches the wire, the collar gives the dog a shock.

Though a fence-less containment system may seem like a good way to keep your dog in his yard, it has some serious drawbacks. The system requires an electric power supply to the transmitter and a battery for the collar, and if either of

> **Note:** It's a good idea to warn neighbors that you have added an electric fence wire. Failure to do so may create neighborhood discontent, and perhaps a lawsuit, if a child unwittingly touches the fence and receives a shock. Also check local ordinances to be certain your area allows their use.

those fail, the system stops working. Sometimes the transmitter or receiver can malfunction and give the dog repeated, inescapable shocks even when he's not near the wire. Some dogs will run past the boundary even though they receive shocks when they do. Some dogs develop fear of receiving the shock and refuse to use their yard at all, resulting in house-soiling problems. Some dogs develop aggression related to being confined with electronic containment systems.

Another serious weakness with this type of system is that stray dogs and other animals can cross it at will and attack the contained dog. People intent on stealing or harming your Lab will not be deterred by the non-fence containment system. These systems also offer no deterrent if neighbor children decide to enter the yard to play with the contained dog. A child may be knocked down or even bitten by the dog, generating disastrous lawsuits against the dog's owner.

A real fence is a more secure method of containing your Lab than an electronic shock-type system. If you live in an area where real fences are not allowed, an electronic system may be the only option for keeping your Lab in your yard. If you do choose to use electronic containment, consider the drawbacks and do all you can to protect Buddy from the many ways this method could fail.

Boredom Causes Misbehavior

Fences, even super-secure ones, are no substitute for attention, exercise, and training. If a dog is left alone too much, he will seek his own entertainment. If there's not enough to keep him busy at home, a bored, smart, underexercised dog will spend his days figuring ways to climb, chew, or tunnel to freedom. Digging, barking, property destruction, fence aggression, and escape attempts are signs that a dog needs more to occupy him.

It is your responsibility to find outlets for Buddy's physical and mental energies. Put his mind and body to work learning basic obedience, then progress to training in agility, tracking, hunting, conformation, musical freestyle, field events, or pet therapy. There are many interesting activities a well-trained dog can enjoy with his handler. Give Buddy a positive way to use his energy and you may hear neighbors praising him instead of complaining.

Borders and Quarantines

Before you travel anywhere with Buddy, find out first which vaccinations and certificates are required at your planned destina-

tion. At home Buddy may be current and legal, but other places may have different regulations. A 3-year rabies vaccination is considered expired after 12 months in countries, states, counties, or cities where yearly vaccination is mandated. Hawaii has a quarantine ranging up to 120 days in length unless the dog meets a number of stringent requirements. These requirements include having been vaccinated for rabies at least twice in its lifetime, a recent blood test for rabies, a veterinary health certificate, and several other documents. Dogs meeting the requirements may be permitted to enter Hawaii without undergoing the 120-day quarantine.

There is a six-month quarantine for dogs entering the United Kingdom, unless the dog is eligible for the Pet Travel Scheme (PETS). To be eligible, the dog must have been vaccinated for rabies within a specified period and be traveling from a European Union (EU) country or certain other approved nations, which now include mainland USA and Hawaii, Canada, Japan, and a number of other countries.

Japan, Australia, and other rabies-free countries each have different quarantine laws for dogs and other animals. If you are thinking of taking Buddy with you to another country, be sure to check all pertinent regulations at least six months before your planned travel date.

Quarantine periods vary, but are considered necessary to prevent island inhabitants from becoming infected by rabid newcomers. With modern advances in immunology, border quarantines may seem a bit archaic, but rabies truly is a serious concern. The disease is 100 percent fatal and can be passed from animals to

If you give your Lab quality care, keep him fit and healthy, and provide friendship, he should prove to be a well-behaved companion.

humans. For this reason, keep Buddy's rabies vaccination up to date, whether or not you plan any border crossings.

Protecting Your Lab

An ID tag can be lost, so, as discussed on page 30, it's safest to have Buddy tattooed and/or microchipped for identification and to help prove ownership. Not only must we protect our dogs from loss, danger, and disease, but we must also protect them from breaking laws. Dog bites are the big legal problems, but even the friendliest Lab could cause property damage or accidentally injure someone. Responsible owners can prevent most potential doggie disasters with a bit of forethought.

Most Labs are friendly and happy, but any dog could become self-protective when frightened. The best way to protect Buddy from fear reactions is to familiarize him with all kinds of people, animals,

sights, sounds, and smells. If he learns to accept these as normal, he will not tend to be as afraid or defensive.

Take Buddy through puppy class, then basic obedience, then advanced training. He will then have such good manners that you'll be able to take him almost any-where. Keep him fit and healthy with regular exercise and good grooming. A dog that receives quality care and friendship on a daily basis is calmer, healthier, and feels better, and does not tend to behave in ways that bring legal trouble.

Train Buddy, fence him securely, leash him when away from home, and crate him for travel. Vaccinate him, keep him healthy and clean, take him interesting places, and introduce him to friendly adults and children.

Teach Buddy to trust you to keep him safe, no matter what, then never betray that trust. That kind of responsible owner attitude will keep you and Buddy on the right side of the law.

Temperament and Intelligence Tests

Puppy Temperament Test

1. Cradle the pup on his back. Hold gently, yet firmly, and stroke pup's chest.

   a. Pup immediately freezes and may avert his eyes.
   b. Pup first squirms, then relaxes to enjoy gentle petting.
   c. Pup fights vigorously to right himself, may vocalize or bite.

2. Gently restrain pup and tickle the pad surface of rear foot for ten seconds.

   a. Pup reacts little, if at all. May seem to enjoy the feeling.
   b. Pup wiggles and kicks foot against tickle.
   c. Pup tries to escape by squirming away, may bite.

3. Rapidly bang five times on the bottom of a steel pan with a wooden spoon.

   a. Pup freezes or runs, may try to hide, may urinate. Remains anxious afterwards.
   b. Pup startles slightly then seeks source of sound.
   c. Pup faces sound and barks. Hair on shoulders may stand erect.

4. Press palm of hand against pup's chest, as a barrier.

   a. Pup backs up or sits down.
   b. Pup leans into hand with matching pressure.
   c. Pup pushes through, around, over, or under barrier, may paw and bite.

5. Suddenly flap a small towel up and down several times about a foot from the pup's face.

   a. Pup dodges away, does not approach.
   b. Pup flinches or ducks, then becomes curious.
   c. Pup tries to grab the towel.

PUPPY TEMPERAMENT TEST (© 1999 September B. Morn)

6. Sit on the floor and begin eating a snack. If the pup crowds in, hoping for a taste, gently but firmly push him away.

   a. Pup does not crowd in at all.
   b. Pup crowds in but yields to your push away after three or four times.
   c. Pup continues to crowd for food and will not yield.

Scoring Directions

Add scores: a = 1, b = 2, c = 3

Interpreting Your Puppy's Score

6 or 7: Indicates an overly timid pup. This pup will need a regular schedule with few surprises, a calm home environment, and a great deal of encouragement. This is not a good puppy for a busy owner and may be too self-protective to be around children.

8 to 10: A submissive and sensitive pup. With patience and gentle handling, this pup can be easily trained. Education should start with puppy kindergarten socialization and continue until at least one and a half years of age in reward-based training classes. This could be a good family dog around well-behaved, gentle children but probably not rowdy or boisterous ones.

11 to 13: Pup has normal reactions to both temptation and limitation. Reward-based training will help this curious and responsive pup learn the rules of your household. This pup will do best when he understands what you want. If socialized with children while young, this dog will enjoy their company and games.

14 to 16: Indicates a confident pup, curious about the world and eager to interact with it. This pup should receive obedience training as a youngster, then go on to further education. A pup with this temperament should do well in any kind of sport or competition that physically suits him.

17 or 18: Pup is overly bold and physically reactive. This pup would not do well with children, non-assertive adults, or first-time dog owners. This pup may learn early that he can intimidate people, which must not be permitted to happen as, once formed, the habit is difficult to cure. Professional training advice should be sought if your puppy scores this high.

Puppy I.Q. Test

1. Puppy likes to carry objects around

     a. seldom or never
     b. only food items
     c. food and favorite toys only
     d. most everything he can find

2. Puppy uses front paws

     a. only to walk and run
     b. to paw objects in play
     c. to hold objects
     d. to reach objects that have rolled under furniture

3. When puppy hears an unfamiliar sound, he

     a. runs and hides
     b. runs away, then looks for the source
     c. looks at where sound came from, may bark, but does not approach
     d. approaches source of sound

4. When you roll a ball or toy past puppy, he

     a. seems not to notice
     b. watches it go by, but does not follow
     c. follows object and plays with it
     d. brings object to you (may or may not release)

PUPPY I.Q. TEST (© 1999 September B. Morn)

5. When puppy sees someone he has played with before, he will

   a. not approach
   b. approach tentatively
   c. approach and greet person happily
   d. attempt to play with person as on former visit (bring same toy, start similar game, and so on)

6. When you show puppy a toy, then conceal it under a towel, he

   a. loses interest
   b. looks at you, may whine or bark
   c. sniffs towel, then looks at you
   d. attempts to find the object under the towel

Scoring Directions

a = 5, b = 10, c = 15, d = 20

1. Add scores.
2. Subtract the puppy's age in weeks. *(Note: If pup is older than 26 weeks, use 26 to represent age when calculating score.)*
3. Multiply by 2 to get "Puppy I.Q."

Interpreting Your Puppy's Score

0 to 50: This pup will need encouragement and gentle repetition to learn commands and manners. Take walks together and play cooperation games, but wait until this pup has confidence in your leadership to enroll in formal classes. Trained and socialized gently and patiently, this puppy will develop few bad habits and should grow up to be a sweet and loving friend.

51 to 100: This pup may enjoy active games, especially with gentle children and adults. He will enjoy training most when rewards are consistent and discipline is low-key. Help this pup succeed and let him savor success before going on to a new lesson. This will be a fun and lovable buddy dog when gently trained and socialized.

101 to 150: This pup is clever and takes well to training. A let's-have-fun approach to lessons is best. Obedience competition, Agility, and Tracking may be enjoyable for this pup. Expect some impish disobedience at times; this pup may invent alternatives to the usual routine, so try to keep your sense of humor. This pup will be a charming companion when trained with positive methods and well socialized.

151 or more: Lucky you, your puppy is a genius! Enroll in Puppy Kindergarten as early as possible. Be sure all training is gentle and positive, as this pup will develop a sour attitude if overworked or overdisciplined. Build puppy's mind and body with games and sports as well as obedience training. He will be able to learn anything you're clever enough to teach. This pup may at times be a real challenge to your wits, but with proper socialization and training, will be the most delightful of canine companions.

Useful Addresses and Literature

Books

Alexander, Melissa. *Click for Joy!* Waltham, MA: Sunshine Books, 2003.

Barry, Jim, Emmen, Mary and Susan Smith. *Positive Gun Dogs—Clicker Training for Sporting Breeds.* Waltham, MA: Sunshine Books, 2007.

Coile, Caroline D. *Beyond Fetch—Fun, Interactive Activities for You and Your Dog.* New York: Howell Book House, 2003.

Dennison, Pamela. *Click Your Way to Rally Obedience.* Loveland, CO: Alpine Publishing, 2006.

Laurence, Kay. *Learning Games.* Waltham, MA: Sunshine Books, 2008.

McAuliffe, Claudeen. *The Big Bang! How You Can Help Your Dog Cope With Thunderstorms and Fireworks.* Oconomowoc, WI: Kindness Canine Behavior Consultants, LLC, 2006.

McConnell, Patricia. *Cautious Canine,* 2nd ed. Madison, WI: Dog's Best Friend, 2005.

Pelar, Colleen. *Living With Kids and Dogs... Without Losing Your Mind.* Woodbridge, VA: C & R Publishing, 2007.

Pitcairn, Richard, and Susan Pitcairn. *Dr. Pitcairn's Complete Guide To Natural Health For Dogs & Cats,* 3rd ed. Emmaus, PA: Rodale Press, 2005.

Rice, Dan. *The Complete Book of Dog Breeding,* 2nd ed. Hauppauge, NY: Barron's Educational Series, Inc., 2008.

Rugaas, Turid. *On Talking Terms With Dogs,* 2nd ed. Wenatchee, WA: Dogwise Publishing, 2006.

Shojai, Amy. *First Aid Companion for Dogs & Cats.* Emmaus, PA: Rodale Press, 2001.

Silvani, Pia, and Lynn Eckhardt. *Raising Puppies and Kids Together—A Guide for Parents.* Neptune, NJ: TFH, 2005.

Smith, Cheryl. *Visiting the Dog Park— Having Fun, Staying Safe.* Wenatchee, WA: Dogwise Publishing, 2007.

Tarrant, Bill. *Hey Pup, Fetch It Up: The Complete Retriever Training Book.* Mechanicsburg, PA: Stackpole Books, 1993.

Yin, Sophia. *How to Behave So Your Dog Behaves.* Neptune, NJ: TFH, 2004.

Organizations

American Kennel Club
5580 Centerview Drive, Suite 200
Raleigh, NC 27606
(919) 233-9767
www.akc.org

United Kennel Club
100 East Kilgore Road
Kalamazoo, MI 49001-5593
(616) 343-9020
www.ukcdogs.com

Canadian Kennel Club
89 Skyway Avenue, Suite 100
Etobicoke, Ontario
Canada M9W 6R4
(416) 675-5511; (416) 250-8040
Fax: (416) 675-6506
www.ckc.ca

Federation Cynologique Internationale
(International Kennel Club)
13, Place Albert 1
B-6530 Thuin
Belgium
(011) 3271591238
www.fci.be/home.asp?lang=en

The Kennel Club (United Kingdom)
1-5 Clarges Street
Picadilly
London W1Y 8AB England
(011) 44 171 629 5828
Fax: (011) 44 171 518 1028
www.thekennelclub.org.uk

Behavior/Training

American Veterinary Society of Animal
  Behavior
E-mail: *avsabe@yahoo.com*
www.avsabonline.org

American Temperament Test Society
P.O. Box 800130
Balch Springs, TX 75180
(972) 557-2887
www.atts.org

Association of Pet Dog Trainers
150 Executive Center Drive, Box 35
Greenville, SC 29615
1-800-738-3647
www.apdt.com

National Association of Dog Obedience
  Instructors
P.O. Box 432
Landing, NJ 077850
www.nadoi.org

Breed Associations

Labrador Retriever Club of America
1221 Hidden Cove Ct.
Granbury, TX 76049
www.thelabradorclub.com

Hunting Retriever Club
P.O. Box 3179
Big Spring, TX 79721-3179
(915) 267-1659
Fax: (915) 267-1650
www.hrc-ukc.com

Rescue

Labrador Retriever Club
Rescue Coordinator
Luanne Lindsey
1320 County Road 272
Leander, TX 78641
(512) 259-3645
Fax: (512) 259-5227
E-mail: applyland@texas.net

Sporting Activities

Canine Freestyle Federation
www.canine-freestyle.org

International Disc Dog Handlers
    Association
1690 Julius Bridge Road
Ball Ground, GA 30107
(770) 735-6200
www.iddha.com

International Weight Pull Association
E-mail: info@iwpa.net
www.iwpa.net

North American Skijoring and Ski Pulk
    Association
P.O. Box 240573
Anchorage, AK 99524
(907) 349-WOOF

North American Dog Agility Council
P.O. Box 1206
Colbert, OK 74733
E-mail: info@nadac.com
www.nadac.com

North American Flyball Association
1400 West Devon Avenue, #512
Chicago, IL 60660
(800) 318-6312 (phone and fax)
E-mail: flyball@flyball.org
www.flyball.org

United States Dog Agility Association
P.O. Box 850955
Richardson, TX 75085-0955
(972) 487-2200
www.usdaa.com

World Canine Freestyle Organization, Ltd.
P.O. Box 350122
Brooklyn, NY 11235
(718) 332-8336
Fax: (718) 646-2686
E-mail: wcfodogs@aol.com
www.worldcaninefreestyle.org

Working Activities

American Rescue Dog Association
P.O. Box 613
Bristow, VA 20136
(888) 775-8871
www.ardainc.org

Delta Society
875 124th Avenue NE, Suite 101
Bellvue, WA 98055-1329
E-mail: info@deltasociety.org
www.deltasociety.org

National Association for Search and
    Rescue (NASAR)
(703) 222-6283
E-mail: info@nasar.org
www.nasar.org

Love On A Leash (Foundation for
   Pet Provided Therapy)
P.O. Box 4115
Oceanside, CA 92052
(760) 740-2326
E-mail: info@loveonaleash.org
www.loveonaleash.org

Therapy Dogs International
88 Bartley Road
Flanders, NJ 07836
(973) 252-9800
E-mail: tdi@gti.net
www.tdi-dog.org

Periodicals and Newsletters

AKC Hunting Test Herald
(Magazine includes training articles,
event schedules, test results)
American Kennel Club
5580 Centerview Drive, Suite 200
Raleigh, NC 27606-33900
(919) 233-9767
www.akc.org

Gun Dog
(Bimonthly magazine; covers training
articles, events, tests and field trials)
P.O. Box 35098
Des Moines, IA 50315-0301
(800) 800-7724
www.gundogmag.com

Hunting Retriever Club Magazine
(Quarterly magazine; free with
membership)
Hunting Retriever Club Inc.
Membership Department
100 East Kilgore Road
Kalamazoo, MI 49002-5592
www.huntingretrieverclub.org

Retriever Field Trial News
(Magazine published jointly by National
Retriever Club and National Amateur
Retriever Club; covers field trials, results,
and reviews)
4213 South Howell Avenue
Milwaukee, WI 53207
(414) 481-2760
www.working-retriever.com

The Lab Connection
(Newsletter included with membership;
articles on training, health, and
competitions)
National Labrador Retriever Club
105 Coles Drive
Doylestown, PA 18901
www.nationallabradorretrieverclub.com

The Retriever Journal
(Bimonthly magazine; columns and
articles on training for hunting)
Wildwood Press
P.O. Box 968
Traverse City, MI 49685
(800) 333-7646

Glossary

Aggression: Combative tendency to guard, protect, or bite.

Agility trial: A timed contest over an obstacle course.

Allbreed show: A conformation event open to all registered breeds.

American Kennel Club (AKC): Official national dog registration organization in United States.

Antibodies: Specialized proteins that body forms to create immunity.

Anxiety: Generalized fear.

Assistance dog: Dog trained to assist people with disabilities.

Attention: Mental concentration.

Attention training: Training the dog to concentrate on cues from the handler.

Attitude: Disposition or mental set.

Authority figure: One with the power and right to give commands.

Automatic *sit*: Dog sits at heel without command when handler stops moving.

Baby gate: A folding barrier used to block the lower portion of a doorway.

Behavior: Conduct, manners, response to the environment.

Best in Show: The dog that defeats all others at a conformation event.

Boat bumper: A flexible plastic or canvas cylinder used to protect a boat from rubbing against a dock; also used as a floating fetch object in dog training.

Body language: Communication that depends on physical postures and gestures.

Bonding: Forming a relationship.

Breed Standard: An official written standard of perfection, describing the ideal dog of a particular breed.

Calming signals: Body language such as yawning, which sends a noncombative message.

Canine Good Citizen (CGC): AKC program certifying dogs that pass an official test of good public manners.

Carting: Dog sport or work of pulling a cart, in harness.

Champion: Conformation title earned with wins at dog shows.

Chase response: Natural tendency of dogs to go after moving things.

Chew toy: A toy designed for dogs to safely chew.

Command: A word or phrase that signals a dog to do a task.

Conformation: The shape and symmetry of an animal's body.

Correction: In training this refers to an action by the handler that helps the dog do right after it has disobeyed.

Crate: A comfortable wire or plastic cage used to confine a dog for short periods.

Crate-train: To teach a dog to accept confinement.

Customs dog: Dog working with Customs officers, detecting contraband at ports and borders.

Den: A dog's cozy sleeping and lounging place.

Dock jumping: A competitive water sport that awards prizes to the dog with the longest and/or highest measured jump into water from a dock.

Dog language: Body language and vocalizations used to communicate among dogs.

Dog walkathon: An event where sponsored participants walk with their dogs to raise money for charity.

Dominant: This is a relative term, meaning higher in the pack order than another dog.

Drives: Natural urges that motivate a dog.

Eye contact: Looking directly into another's eyes.

Field stock: Dogs bred to hunt or field trial.

Field trial: An event where dogs demonstrate their hunting skills.

Figure 8: The dog goes around one obstacle, then another, crossing his own track in between, in the approximate shape of the number eight.

Finish to heel: The dog moves, on command or signal, from in front of the handler to the handler's left side (heel position).

Flotation vest: A safety device/garment that can help keep a dog from drowning if overtired or injured in deep water.

Flyball: A team relay sport for dogs.

Flying disc: A plastic or cloth disc thrown for dogs to retrieve.

Food-toy: A toy that is partially or completely edible.

Force training: Teaching a dog by physically forcing it into position.

Freestyle (musical): The sport of musical heelwork and dancing with dogs.

Guide dog: Assistance dog that leads the blind.

Gundog: Hunting dog.

Hand signals: Hand and arm gestures that cue a dog's behavior.

Hearing dog: Assistance dog that alerts hearing-impaired human partner to sounds.

Heel: Position of dog with neck close beside, but not touching, handler's left leg.

Hierarchy: The dominance/submission spectrum.

Hormones: A body substance that affects the workings of organ systems.

Immune system: The system that protects the body from disease by forming antibodies.

Incontinence: Inability to control release of urine from the bladder.

Life ring: A floating ring used in water rescues.

Long line: A leash or rope from 10 to 100 feet (3 to 30 m) in length.

Lure: An attractant, like food or toys, used to motivate a dog to act a certain way.

Marking: Urinating or defecating (less common) to scent and claim territory.

Microchip: A tiny coded chip injected under animal's skin as identification.

Motivation: Anything that makes a dog do something.

Mouthy: Nippy, bitey, licky, etc.

Mushing: Sport of snow sled racing.

Neutering: Inactivation of reproductive capability.

Newfoundland dog: Large, longhaired water dog related to Labrador Retriever.

Obedience trial: Competition where dogs earn titles by completing test routines.

Off-leash park: Area of park designated for off-leash dog exercise and training.

Pack leader: The dog or person a dog relies on for direction and protection.

Pet door: Small opening with closing flap installed in door or wall for pet access.

Pedigree: Written record of a dog's ancestry.

Performance dog: Dog that competes in canine sporting events.

Pet quality: Dog has minor, nondisabling, conformation faults.

Posture: Body position; used by dogs as indication of rank.

Praise: Happy words that handler uses when dog does well.

Punishment: Unpleasant consequences for performing a behavior that will discourage the dog from repeating that behavior in the future.

Puppy corral: Small safe enclosure inside or outdoors where pup is kept when unattended.

Puppy kindergarten: Classes in good manners and social skills for young pups.

Puppy pushups: *Sit*, then *down*, then *sit*, then *down*, then *sit*, etc.

Puppy raiser: A person who raises and trains an assistance dog candidate pup until it is ready for formal schooling.

Quarantine: Enforced separation of an animal from others for a period of time to determine its health and protect others from communicable disease.

Rally: A competitive event in which the dog and handler heel around a course of numbered stations, performing obedience exercises as designated by the printed sign at each station.

Recall exercise: The formal *"Come"* when called; usually includes finish to heel.

Release word: A command that tells a dog an exercise is over.

Relief area: Place for the dog to eliminate waste.

Repetition: Doing something over and over; this is important for the dog to learn it.

Reputable breeder: A knowledgeable, ethical person who produces purebred, registered dogs with the ideal of improving the breed.

Reward: Pleasant consequences for performing a behavior that will encourage the dog to repeat that behavior in the future.

Reward-based training: Training based on the dog earning rewards rather than on avoiding punishments.

St. John's water dog: The early name for the Labrador Retriever.

Search and Rescue (SAR): Use of tracking dogs to search for lost or missing hikers, etc.

Search dog: A dog that searches by scent for lost people.

Seizure alert dog: Assistance dog that indicates an approaching seizure and gives comfort afterward.

Sensitive periods: Emotionally sensitive periods when pup is more fearful than usual.

Service dog: Assistance dog trained to help an individual with a physical or mental disability.

Show stock: Dogs raised to conform to show standards.

Signal: Nonverbal command; can be with hand, whistle, etc.

Skijoring: Dog in harness pulls cross-country skier over snow.

Socialization: Introducing dog in a positive way to people, animals, and situations.

Spaying: Surgical removal of a female dog's reproductive organs.

Specialty show: Competitive event limited to one breed only.

Sporting group: One of seven AKC classification groups; Retrievers, Setters, Pointers, and Spaniels are in this group.

Staring: Prolonged eye contact; perceived by most dogs as threatening.

Stress: Mental or physical tension or strain.

Styptic: Astringent substance that stops bleeding.

Submissive: Lower than another in the hierarchy.

Tattoo: Permanent identifying mark made by injecting pigment under the skin surface.

Temperament: Natural disposition.

Therapy dog: Trained, socialized dog that brings comfort to patients at care facilities.

Tie-out: A tether for a dog outdoors.

Tracking: Following a scent left on the ground by a passing person or animal.

Trashing: Destructively making a mess when left alone.

Treat: A food reward.

Trust training: Gentle exercises that build a dog's confidence in his handler.

Underdog: Dog at the bottom of the pack hierarchy.

Upland game: Field birds and animals hunted for sport.

Waterfowl: Birds that can swim.

Index